The Two Covenants

ANDREW MURRAY

CLC ❖ PUBLICATIONS
Fort Washington, Pennsylvania 19034

Published by CLC ❖ Publications

U.S.A.
P.O. Box 1449, Fort Washington, PA 19034

GREAT BRITAIN
51 The Dean, Alresford, Hants. SO24 9BJ

AUSTRALIA
P.O. Box 419M, Manunda, QLD 4879

NEW ZEALAND
10 MacArthur Street, Feilding

ISBN 0-87508-782-5

Copyright © 2005
CLC Ministries International

This American Trade Paper edition 2005
Edited by Robert Delancy

Updated New American Standard Bible
© 1995 by the Lockman Foundation.
Used by permission.

Text set in *Garamond*

This printing 2005

Contents

Chapter 1 • A Covenant God • 11

Chapter 2 • The Two Covenants: Their Relation • 17

Chapter 3 • The First Covenant • 23

Chapter 4 • The New Covenant • 29

Chapter 5 • The Two Covenants—In Christian Experience • 35

Chapter 6 • The Everlasting Covenant • 43

Chapter 7 • The New Covenant: A Ministry of the Spirit • 51

Chapter 8 • The Two Covenants: The Transition • 57

Chapter 9 • The Blood of the Covenant • 65

Chapter 10 • Jesus, the Mediator of the New Covenant • 71

Chapter 11 • Jesus, the Guarantor of a Better Covenant • 77

Chapter 12 • The Book of the Covenant • 83

Chapter 13 • New Covenant Obedience • 89

Chapter 14 • The New Covenant: A Covenant of Grace • 97

Chapter 15 • The Covenant of a Perpetual Priesthood • 103

Chapter 16 • The Ministry of the New Covenant • 109

Chapter 17 • His Holy Covenant • 115

Chapter 18 • Entering the Covenant: With All the Heart • 121

Note A: The Second Blessing • 129

Note B: The Law Written on the Heart • 134

Note C: George Müller and His Second Conversion • 138

Note D: Canon Battersby • 144

Note E: Nothing of Myself • 147

Note F: The Whole Heart • 150

Introduction

ONE of the recognized goals for any preacher of God's Word is to take the sacred text, originally written for the people of another culture who lived centuries ago, and make it clear and understandable for one's contemporaries. And a worthy aim this is. But if this is one's only goal and is all he accomplishes—a mere enlightening of the mind—in God's sight his ministry is a failure. If a minister is to be faithful to the One who has sent him, he must be sure to challenge his hearers to apply the message of the Spirit to their daily lives—to live vigorously and consistently according to the divine prescription. And such is my intent.

One of the words of Scripture that seems to have gone out of fashion is the word "covenant." There was a time when it was the keynote of our theology and of the Christian life of strong and holy men. We know how deeply in Scotland it entered into the national life and thought. It made mighty men, to whom God and His promises of power were wonderfully real. It will be found still to bring strength and purpose to those who are willing to place their entire life under the control of God. The inspiring assurance that they are living in covenant with a God who has sworn to fulfill in them His every promise will make them mighty too.

This book is a humble attempt to show exactly what the blessings are that God has covenanted to bestow on us; what assurance the Covenant gives us that the blessings can and will be fulfilled; what the position is that it gives us with God Himself; and, what the conditions are for the full and continual experience of its blessings. I feel confident that if I can lead any to listen to what God has to say about His Covenant, and to deal with Him as a Covenantal God, it will bring them both strength and joy.

Not long ago I received a letter containing the following suggestions: "I think you will excuse and understand me when I say there is one further note of power I would like so much to have introduced into your next book on Intercession. God Himself has, I know, been giving me some direct teaching this winter on the place the New Covenant is to have in intercessory prayer. . . . I know you believe in the Covenant and the Covenant rights we have flowing from it. Have you followed through on your views of the Covenant as they bear upon this subject of intercession? Am I wrong in coming to the conclusion that we may come boldly into God's presence and not only ask but also claim a Covenant right through Christ Jesus to all the spiritual searching, and cleansing, and knowledge, and power promised in the three great Covenant promises? If you would take the Covenant and speak of it as God could enable you to speak, I think that would be the quickest way the Lord could take to wake up His Church to the power He has put into our hands by giving us a Covenant. I would be so glad if you would tell God's people that they have a Covenant."

Though this letter was not the occasion of the writing of

the book, and our Covenant rights have been considered elsewhere in a far wider aspect in their relation to prayer, I am persuaded that nothing will help us more in our work of intercession than the entrance for ourselves personally into what it means that *we have a Covenant God.*

My one great desire has been to ask Christians whether they are really seeking to find out what exactly God wants them to be and is willing to make them! It is only as they wait for "the mind of the Lord to be shown them" that their faith can ever truly see, or accept, or enjoy what God calls "His salvation." As long as we expect God to do for us what we ask or think, we limit Him. When we believe that as high as the heavens are above the earth so His thoughts are above our thoughts, and wait on Him as *God* to do unto us *according to His Word*, as *He* means it, we shall be prepared to live the truly supernatural, heavenly life the Holy Spirit can work in us—the true *Christ-life.*

May God lead every reader into the secret of His presence and *show him His Covenant.*

Andrew Murray
Wellington, South Africa
1st November 1898

Chapter

1

A Covenant God

"Know therefore that the Lord your God, He is God, the faithful God, who keeps His covenant and His lovingkindness to a thousand generations with those who love Him and keep His commandments." —Deut. 7:9.

MEN often make covenants. They know the advantages to be derived from them. A covenant can bring an end to enmity between two parties. It can spell out a list of services and benefits that are to be rendered by the parties, offering security for their certain performance. As a bond of friendship and goodwill, as a ground for perfect confidence, a covenant has often been of unspeakable value.

In His infinite condescension to our human weakness and need, God has sought to make use of every possible means to give us perfect confidence in Himself, and full assurance of all that He, in His infinite riches and power as God, has promised to do for us. It is with this in view that He has consented to bind Himself by covenant, as if He could not be trusted. Happy is the person who truly knows God as his Covenant God and understands what the Covenant promises him. What an unwavering confidence of expectation it secures, guaranteeing that all its terms will be fulfilled to him! What a claim and hold it gives him on the Covenant-keeping God Himself! To many a person who has never thought much about the Covenant, a true and living faith in it would mean the transformation of his whole life. The full knowledge of what God wants to do for him and the assurance that He will certainly do it makes the Covenant the very gate of heaven. May the Holy Spirit give us insight into some of its glory.

When God created man in His image and likeness His intent was that man might have a life as much like His own as it was possible for a creature to have. This was to be by God Himself living and working in man. His desire was that man would yield himself in loving dependence to the wonderful glory of being the recipient, the bearer, the manifestation of the divine life. The one secret of man's happiness was to be a trustful surrender of his whole being to the willing and the working of God. When sin entered, this relationship to God was destroyed, for when man disobeyed, he feared God and fled from Him. He no longer knew, or loved, or trusted God.

Man could not save himself from the power of sin. If his redemption was to be effected, God must do it all. And if God was to do it in harmony with the law of man's nature, man must be brought to desire it—to give his willing consent and entrust himself to God. All that God wanted man to do was to believe in Him. What a man believes moves and rules his whole being, for it enters into him and becomes part of his very life. Salvation could only be by faith. Only God could restore the life man had lost; so man must in faith yield himself to God's work and will. The first great work of God with man was to get him to believe. This work cost God more care and time and patience than we can easily conceive. All His dealings with individual men and with the people of Israel had just this one object: to teach men to trust Him. Where He found faith He could do anything. Nothing dishonored and grieved Him so much as unbelief. Unbelief was the root of disobedience and of every sin; it made it impossible for God to do His work. The one thing God sought to waken in men by promise and threatening, by mercy and judgment, was faith.

Of the many devices that God's patient and condescending grace made use of to stir up and strengthen faith, the chief was the Covenant. In more than one way God sought to accomplish this by His Covenant. First of all, His Covenant was always *a revelation of His purposes*, for it set forth in definite promises what God was willing to bring about in those with whom the Covenant was made. It was a divine outline and pattern of the work God intended to do on their behalf so that they might know what to desire and expect. Thus, their faith might nourish itself with the very things, though as yet unseen, that God was working out. Likewise, the Covenant was meant to be *a security and guarantee*, as simple and understandable as the divine glory could make it, that the very things that God had promised would indeed be brought to pass in those with whom He had entered into covenant. Amid all delay and disappointment and apparent failure of the divine promises, the Covenant was to be the anchor of the soul, a pledge of the divine truthfulness and faithfulness and unchangeableness for the performance of what had been promised. And so the Covenant was, above all, designed to give man *a hold upon God* as the Covenant-keeping One. It was to link him to God Himself in expectation and hope—to bring him to make God Himself alone the portion and the strength of his soul.

Oh, that we knew how God longs that we should trust Him, and how surely His every promise must be fulfilled for those who do so! Oh, that we knew how it is owing to nothing but our unbelief that we cannot enter into the possession of God's promises, and that without our trust God cannot—yes, cannot—do His mighty works in us and for us and through us! Oh, that we knew how one of the surest remedies for our unbelief—the divinely chosen cure for it—is the Covenant into which God has entered with us! The sending forth of the Spirit, the economy of grace in Christ Jesus, the whole of our spiritual life, the health and growth and strength of the Church, has been provided for and secured in the New Covenant. Is it any wonder that where that Covenant is little thought of, where its plea for an abounding and unhesitating confidence in God is little understood and tested, that the Christian misses the joy, the strength. the holiness and the heavenliness which God intended and so clearly promised that he should have.

Let us listen to the words in which God's written revelation calls us to know and worship and trust our Covenant-keeping God. Hopefully we shall find what we have been looking for: the deep, full experience of all that God's grace can do in us. In our text Moses says: "*Know therefore* that the Lord your God, He is God, *the faithful God, who keeps His covenant* and His lovingkindness . . . with those who love Him." Hear also what God says in Isaiah 54:10: "The mountains may be removed and the hills may shake, but My lovingkindness will not be removed from you, and *My covenant of peace will not be shaken.*" More sure than any mountain is the fulfillment of every Covenant promise. And in Jeremiah 32:40 God speaks of a *New* Covenant: "*I will make an everlasting covenant with them that I will not turn away from them*, to do them good; and I will put the fear of Me in their hearts so that they will not turn away from Me." This Covenant assures us that God will not turn away from us nor we turn away from Him—that He undertakes both for Himself and for us.

Let us ask very earnestly whether the lack in our Christian life, and especially in our faith, is not owing to our neglect of the Covenant. Perhaps we have not trusted the Covenant-keeping God. Our soul has not done what God called us to do—to "take hold of His Covenant," to "remember the Covenant." So God could not fulfill His promises in us. We need to examine the terms of the Covenant, to see it as the title-deed of our inheritance—of the riches we are to possess even here on earth. We need to think of the certainty of its fulfillment, more sure than the foundations of the everlasting mountains. If we will turn to the God who keeps His Covenant forever, our life will surely be transformed. It can and will be all that God would make it.

The great lack of our spiritual life is that we need more of God. We have accepted salvation as His gift, but we have not comprehended that the object of our salvation—and its chief blessing—is to bring us into that *close relationship with God* for which we were created and in which our glory in eternity will be found. All that God has done in making a covenant for His people is designed to teach them to trust in Him, to delight in Him, to be one with Him. It cannot be otherwise. If God is, indeed, the very fountain of goodness and glory, of beauty and blessedness, the more we have of His presence, the more we conform to His will, the more we are engaged in His service, the more we have Him ruling and working in us, the more truly happy we shall be. If God is, indeed, the owner and author of life and strength, of holiness and happiness, and can alone give and work this in us, the more we trust and depend on Him the stronger and holier and the happier we shall be. The only *true* life is one that brings us every day nearer to God and makes us give up everything to have more of Him. No obedience can be too strict, no dependence too absolute, no confidence too implicit, to a person who is learning to count God Himself his chief good, his exceeding joy.

In entering into covenant with us, God's one object is to draw us to Himself, to render us entirely dependent upon Himself, and so to bring us into the right position and disposition in which He can fill us with Himself, His love, and His blessedness. Let us undertake our study of the New Covenant with the honest purpose and desire to know what God wishes to be to us and to do in us. The New Covenant will become to us one of the windows of heaven through which we see into the very heart of God.

Chapter

2

—⟡—

The Two Covenants:
Their Relation

"It is written that Abraham had two sons, one by the bond-woman and one by the free woman. But the son by the bond-woman was born according to the flesh, and the son by the free woman through the promise. This is allegorically speaking, for these women are two covenants."—Gal. 4:22–24.

THERE are two Covenants, one called the Old, the other the New. God speaks of this very distinctly in Jeremiah, where He says: "Behold, days are coming when I will make a new covenant with the house of Israel . . . not like the covenant which I made with their fathers" (Jer. 31:31–32). This is quoted in Hebrews 8, with the addition: "When He said, 'A new covenant,' He has made the first obsolete" (v.13). Our Lord Himself spoke of the New Covenant in His blood.

In His dealings with His people, in His working out of His great redemption, it has pleased God that there should be two Covenants. God has not done this arbitrarily but for good and wise purposes which made it indispensably necessary that it should be so and not otherwise. The clearer our insight into the reasons for there being two Covenants, and into their relation to each other, the more full and true can be our personal apprehension of what the New Covenant is meant to be to us. These Covenants indicate two stages in God's dealing with man and two ways of our serving God: a lower or elementary one of preparation and promise, a higher or more advanced one of fulfillment and possession. As the true excellency of the second is opened up to us, we can spiritually enter into what God has prepared for us.

Let us try to understand why there should have been two Covenants, neither less nor more.

The reason for two Covenants is that in any interaction between God and man there are two parties, and each of these must have the opportunity to prove what his part in the Covenant is. In the Old Covenant man was given the opportunity to prove what he could do, with the aid of all the means of grace God could bestow. That Covenant ended in man proving his own unfaithfulness and failure. In the New Covenant, God is to prove what *He* can do with man, as unfaithful and feeble as he is, when He is allowed and trusted to do *all* the work. The Old Covenant was one dependent on man's obedience, one which he could break and *did* break (Jer. 31:32). The New Covenant is one which God has promised shall never be broken, for *He Himself keeps it and ensures our keeping it*. He makes it *an everlasting Covenant*.

It will repay us richly to look a little deeper into this. This relation of God to fallen man in covenant is the same as was His relation to unfallen man as Creator. And what was that relation? God proposed to make man in His own image and likeness. The chief glory of God is that He has *life in Himself*—that He is independent of all else, and owes what He is to Himself alone. If the image and likeness of God was not to be in name only—a sham—and man was really to be like God in the power to make himself what he was to be, he must be given the power of *free will* and *self-determination*. This was the problem God had to solve when He created man in His image. Man was to be a creature made by God; and yet he was to be, as far as a creature could be, like God, *self-made*. In all God's treatment of man these two factors were ever to be taken into account. God was always to take the *initiative* and to be to man the source of life. Man was ever to be the *recipient*, and yet at the same time the disposer of the life God bestowed.

When man fell because of sin and God entered into a covenant of salvation, these two sides of the relationship still had to be maintained intact. God was ever to be the first party and man the second. And yet man, being made in God's image, was always to have full opportunity to appropriate or reject what God gave, to prove how far he could help himself and indeed be self-made. His absolute dependence upon God was not to be forced upon him; if it was really to be a thing of moral worth and true blessedness, it must be by his deliberate and voluntary choice. And this, now, is the reason why there was a first and a second Covenant. In the first, the purpose was that man's desires and efforts might be fully awakened. Time would be given for him to make full proof of what his human nature, with the aid of outward instructions and miracles and means of grace, could accomplish. When his utter impotence, his hopeless captivity under the power of sin had been made plain, there came the New Covenant, in which God would reveal how man's true nobility and Godlikeness was to be found in his absolute *de-*

pendence upon God's being and doing all within him.

In the very nature of things this was the only possible way for God to deal with a being whom He had endowed with the Godlike power of a will. And this is as true in God's dealing with His people as a whole as in dealing with individuals. The two Covenants represent two stages of God's education of man and of man's seeking after God. The progress and transition from the one to the other is not merely chronological or historical, it is organic and spiritual. In greater or lesser degree it is seen in every member of the body as well as in the body as a whole. Under the Old Covenant there were men in whom, by anticipation, the powers of the coming redemption worked mightily. In the New Covenant there are men in whom the spirit of the Old still makes itself manifest. The New Testament gives evidence, in some of its most important epistles—especially those to the Galatians, Romans, and Hebrews—how possible it is within the New Covenant still to be held fast in the bondage of the Old.

This is the teaching of the passage from which our text is taken. In the home of Abraham, the father of the faithful, Ishmael and Isaac are both found: the one born of a slave, the other of a free woman; the one according to the flesh and the will of man, the other through the promise and the power of God; the one only for a time, then to be cast out, the other to be heir of all. This was a picture held up to the Galatians of the life they were leading, for they trusted in the flesh and its religion. Though outwardly they were doing quite well, yet they proved by their being led captive to sin to be not of the free but of the bond woman. Only through faith in the promise and the mighty quickening power of God could they be made truly and fully free and stand in the freedom with which Christ has made us free.

As we proceed to study the two Covenants in the light of this and other scriptures, we shall see how they are indeed the divine revelation of two systems of religious worship, each with its spirit or life-principle, ruling every man who professes to be a Christian. We shall see how the one great cause of the feebleness of so many Christians is that the Old Covenant spirit of bondage still has the mastery. And we shall see that nothing but spiritual insight, with a wholehearted acceptance and a living experience of all the New Covenant promises that *God will work in us,* can possibly fit us for walking as God would desire.

This truth that there are two stages in our service of God, two degrees of nearness in our worship, is typified by many things in the Old Covenant worship, perhaps nowhere more clearly than in the difference between the Holy Place and the Most Holy Place in the temple, with the veil separating them. Into the former the priests could always enter to draw near to God. And yet they might not come too near; the veil kept them at a distance. To pass beyond that was death. Once a year the high priest might enter, as a promise of the time when the veil would be taken away and full access to dwell in God's presence would be given to His people. In Christ's death the veil of the temple was rent, and His blood gives us boldness and power to enter into the Most Holy Place and to live there day by day in the immediate presence of God. It is by the Holy Spirit, who issued forth from that Most Holy Place where Christ had entered to bring God's life to us and to make us one with Him, that we can have the power to live and walk with the consciousness of God's presence in us.

It was, thus, not only in Abraham's home that there were the types of the two Covenants, the spirit of bondage and the spirit of liberty, but even in God's home in the temple. The priests did not yet have liberty of access into the Father's presence. Not only among the Galatians, but throughout the Church there are to be found two classes of Christians. Some are content with the mingled life, half flesh and half spirit, half self-effort and half grace. Others are not content with this but are seeking with their whole heart to know the full deliverance from sin and the abiding power for a walk in God's presence that the New Covenant has brought and can give. May God help us all to be satisfied with nothing less.*

---

* See Note A, on The Second Blessing, page 129.

Chapter

3

The First Covenant

"Now then, if you will indeed obey My voice and keep My covenant, then you shall be My own possession."—Ex. 19:5.

"He declared to you His covenant which He commanded you to perform, that is, the Ten Commandments."—Deut. 4:13.

"Then it shall come about, because you listen to these judgments and keep and do them, that the Lord your God will keep with you His covenant."—Deut. 7:12.

"I will make a new covenant with the house of Israel . . . not like the covenant which I made with their fathers, [even] My covenant which they broke."—Jer. 31:31–32.

W E HAVE seen how the reason for there being two Covenants is to be found in the need of giving the divine and the human will each its due place in the working out of man's destiny. God always takes the initiative. Man must then have the opportunity to do his part and to prove either what he can do or needs to have done for him. The Old Covenant was on the one hand indispensably necessary to awaken man's desires, to call forth his efforts, to deepen his sense of dependence on God, to convince him of his sin and spiritual impotence and thereby prepare him to feel his need for salvation by Christ. In the significant language of Paul: "The law has become our tutor to lead us to Christ" and "We were kept in custody under the law, being shut up to the faith which was later to be revealed" (Gal. 3:24,23). To understand the Old Covenant properly we must always remember its two great characteristics: the one, that it was by divine appointment, accompanied by true blessing, and *absolutely indispensable* for the working out of God's purposes; the other, that it was only temporary and preparatory to something higher, and therefore *absolutely insufficient* for giving the full salvation that man needs if his heart or the heart of God is to be satisfied.

Note now the terms of this first Covenant. "*If you* will indeed obey My voice and keep My covenant . . . you shall be to Me . . . a holy nation" (Ex. 19:5–6). Or, as it is expressed in Jeremiah 7:23, "Obey My voice, and I will be your God." Obedience everywhere, especially in the book of Deuteronomy, appears as the condition of blessing: "A blessing, if you listen to the commandments" (11:27). Some may ask how God could institute a covenant which He knew man could not keep. The answer opens up to us the whole nature and object of the Covenant. All education, divine or human, always deals with its pupils on this principle: faithfulness in the little things is essential to the attainment of the greater. In taking Israel into His training, God dealt with them as men in whom, with all the ruin sin had brought, there was still a conscience to judge between good and evil, a heart capable of being stirred to long after God, and a will to choose the good and ultimately to choose Himself. Before Christ and His salvation could be revealed and understood and truly appreciated, these faculties of man had to be stirred and wakened. The law took men into its training and sought, if I may use the expression, to make them the very best that could be accomplished by external instruction. In the provision made in the law for a symbolical atonement and pardon, in all God's revelation of Himself through priest and prophet and king, in His interposition in providence and grace, everything was done to touch and to win the heart of His chosen people.

Its work was not without fruit. Under the law, administered by the grace that ever accompanied it, there was trained up a number of saints whose great mark was the fear of God and a desire to walk blameless in all His commandments. And yet, as a whole, Scripture represents the Old Covenant as a failure. The law had promised life, but it could not give it (Deut. 4:1; Gal. 3:21). The real purpose for which God had given it was the very opposite: it was meant by Him as "the ministry of death" (2 Cor. 3:7). He gave it that it might convince man of his sin, and might as a result waken the confession of his spiritual impotence and of his need of a New Covenant and a true redemption. It is in this view that Scripture uses such strong expressions as: "Through the law comes *the knowledge of sin*: that *every mouth* may be closed, and all the world may become accountable to God" (Rom. 3:19–20); "The law *brings about wrath*" (Rom. 4:15); "The law came in *so that the transgression would increase*" (Rom. 5:20); "So that through the commandment sin would become *utterly sinful*" (Rom. 7:13); "As many as are of the works of the law are *under a curse*" (Gal. 3:10); "We were kept in custody under the law, being shut up to the faith which was later to be revealed" (Gal. 3:23); "Therefore the law has become our tutor to lead us to Christ, so that we may be justified by faith" (Gal. 3:24). The great work of the law was to reveal what *sin* was: its hatefulness, as cursed by God; its misery, working temporal and eternal ruin; its power, binding man down in hopeless slavery; and the need for a divine intervention as the only hope of deliverance.

In studying the Old Covenant we need to keep in mind this twofold aspect as Scripture represents it. It was God's grace that gave Israel the law, and that grace worked with the law to accomplished its purpose in individual believers and in the people as a whole. The whole of the Old Covenant was a school of grace, an elementary school, to prepare for the fullness of grace and truth in Christ Jesus. A name is generally given to an object according to its chief feature. And so the Old Covenant is called a ministry of *condemnation and death*, not because there was no grace in it—it had its own glory (2 Cor. 3:9–10)—but because the law with its curse was the predominant feature.

The combination of these two aspects we find with special clearness in Paul's epistles. He speaks of all who are "of the works of the law" as being under the curse (Gal. 3:10). And then almost immediately after, he speaks of the law as being our benefactor, a tutor to bring us to Christ, a teacher into whose care we had been given until the time appointed by the Father. We are everywhere brought back to what we said earlier: The Old Covenant is absolutely indispensable for the preparatory work it had to do, but utterly insufficient to work for us a true or a full redemption.

The two great lessons God would teach us by it are very simple. The one is the lesson of *sin*, the other the lesson of *holiness*. The Old Covenant attains its goal only as it brings men to a sense of their utter *sinfulness* and their hopeless inability to deliver themselves. As long as they have not grasped this, no offer of the New Covenant life can lay hold of them. As long as an intense longing for deliverance from sinning has not been achieved, they will naturally fall back into the power of the law and the flesh. The holiness which the New Covenant offers will terrify rather than attract them—largely because the life in the spirit of bondage appears to make more allowance for sin, because obedience is declared to be impossible.

The other is the lesson of *holiness*. In the New Covenant the Triune God promises to do all. He undertakes to give and maintain the new heart, to place His own Spirit in it, to give the will and the power to obey and do His will. As the one demand of the first Covenant was the sense of sin, the one great demand of the New is faith that one's need, created by the discipline of God's law, will be met in a divine and supernatural way. The law cannot work out its purpose unless it brings a man to lie guilty and helpless before the holiness of God. There the New finds him, and reveals that that same God accepts him and makes him a partaker of His holiness.

This book is written for a very practical purpose. Its object is to help believers to *know* the wonderful New Covenant of grace that God has made with them and to lead them into the *daily enjoyment* of the blessed life it secures for them. A practical understanding of the fact that the special work of the first Covenant was to convince of sin, and that without it the New Covenant could not come, is exactly what most Christians need. At conversion they were made aware of sin by the Holy Spirit, but this had reference chiefly to the *guilt* of sin and, in some degree, to its *hatefulness*. But a real knowledge of the *power* of sin—of their utter inability to cast it out and to work in themselves what is good—is what most Christians do not learn at first. And until they have learned this, they cannot possibly enter fully into the blessing of the New Covenant. It is only when a person realizes the impossibility of doing what God demands that he becomes capable of appreciating the New Testament promise and is made willing to wait on God to do all in him.

Do you, my reader, feel that you are not fully living in the New Covenant—that there is still some of the Old Covenant spirit of bondage in you? Then let the Old Covenant finish its work in you. Accept its teaching that all your efforts are failures. As at conversion you were content to fall down as a condemned, death-deserving sinner, be content now to sink down before God in confession that as His redeemed child you still feel yourself utterly unable to do and be what He asks of you. And begin to ask whether the New Covenant has not perhaps a provision you have never yet understood—a provision for meeting your spiritual inability and giving you the strength to do what is well-pleasing to God. You will find the wonderful answer in the assurance that God, by His Holy Spirit, undertakes to work everything in you. The longing to be delivered from the life of daily sinning and the extinction of all hope to secure this by self-effort will prepare us for understanding and accepting God's new way of salvation—*Himself working in us all that is pleasing in His sight.*

Chapter

4

The New Covenant

"'But this is the covenant which I will make with the house of Israel after those days,' declares the Lord, 'I will put My law within them and on their heart I will write it; and I will be their God, and they shall be My people. They will not teach again, each man his neighbor and each man his brother, saying, "Know the Lord," for they will all know Me, from the least of them to the greatest of them,' declares the Lord, 'for I will forgive their iniquity, and their sin I will remember no more.'"—Jer 31:33–34.

I SAIAH has often been called the evangelical prophet because of the wonderful clearness with which he announces the coming Redeemer—both in His humiliation and suffering and in the glory of the kingdom He was to establish. And yet it was given to Jeremiah, in this passage, and to Ezekiel, in the parallel one, to foretell what would actually be the outcome of the Redeemer's work and the essential character of the salvation He was to effect, with a distinctness that is nowhere found in the older prophet. In words that the New Testament (Hebrews 8) takes as the divinely inspired revelation of what the New Covenant is (Christ being the Mediator), God's plan is revealed and we are shown exactly what He will do in us to make us fit and worthy of being His people. Through the whole of the Old Covenant there was always one trouble: man's heart was not right with God. In the New Covenant the evil is to be remedied. Its central promise is a heart delighting in God's law and capable of knowing and maintaining fellowship with Him. Let us note the fourfold blessing spoken of.

1. "*I will put My law within them and on their heart I will write it.*" Let us understand this well. In our heart there are no separate chambers in which the law can be put while the rest of the heart is given up to other things; the heart is a unity. Nor is the heart like a house—which can be filled with things of an entirely different nature from what the walls are made of, without any living organic connection. No, this is speaking of a person's disposition—the love, the will, the life. Nothing can be put into one's heart by God without Him entering and taking possession of it, securing its affection and controlling its whole being. And this is what God undertakes to do by the power of His divine life and operation—to breathe the very spirit of His law into and through the whole inward being. "I will put it within them."

At Sinai the tablets of the Covenant, with the law written on them, were of stone, as a lasting substance. The stone was wholly set apart for this one thing—to carry and show this divine writing. The writing and the stone were inseparably connected. And so the heart in which God gets His way and writes His law in power lives only and wholly to carry that writing and is unchangeably identified with it. Only this way can God realize His purpose in creation and have His child of one mind and one spirit with Himself, delighting in doing His will. When the Old Covenant with the law graven on stone had done its work in the revealing and condemning of sin, the New Covenant would give in its place the life of obedience and true holiness of heart. The entire Covenant blessing centers in this— the heart being made right and equipped to know God: "I will give them *a heart to know Me,* for I am the Lord; and they will be My people, and I will be their God, for they will return to Me *with their whole heart*" (Jer. 24:7).

2. "*And I will be their God, and they shall be My people.*" Do not pass over these words lightly. They occur chiefly in Jeremiah and Ezekiel in connection with the promise of the everlasting Covenant. They express the very highest experience of the Covenant relationship. It is only when God's people learn to love and obey His law, when their hearts and lives are together wholly devoted to Him and His will, that He can be to them the altogether inconceivable blessing that these words express: "*I will be your God.*" He is saying: "All I am and have as God shall be yours. All you can need or wish for in a God, I will be to you. In the fullest meaning of the word, I, the Omnipresent, will be ever present with you, in all My grace and love. I, the Almighty One, will each moment work all in you by My mighty power. I, the Thrice-Holy One, will reveal My sanctifying life within you. I will be your God. *And you shall be My people,* saved and blessed, ruled and guided and provided for by Me, known and seen to be indeed the people of the Holy One, the God of glory." We need to give our hearts time to meditate and wait for the Holy Spirit to work in us all that these words mean.

3. "'*They will not teach again, each man his neighbor and each man his brother, saying, "Know the Lord," for they will all know Me, from the least of them to the greatest of them,*' declares the Lord.*" Individual, personal fellowship with God is to be the

wonderful privilege of every member of the New Covenant people, even the feeblest and the least. Each one will know the Lord. That does not mean the knowledge of the mind but the knowledge that involves appropriation and assimilation and which is eternal life. As the Son knew the Father because He was one with Him and dwelt in Him, the child of God will receive by the Holy Spirit that spiritual illumination which will make God to him the One he knows best, because he loves Him most and lives in Him. The promise "All your sons will be taught of the Lord" (Isa. 54:13; John 6:45) will be fulfilled by the Holy Spirit's teaching. God will speak to each out of His Word what he needs to know.

4. *"For I will forgive their iniquity, and their sin I will remember no more."* The word *for* shows that this is the reason for all that precedes. Because the blood of this New Covenant was of such infinite worth, and its Mediator and High Priest in heaven of such divine power, there is promised through it such a divine blotting out of sin that God cannot remember it. It is this entire blotting out of sin that cleanses and sets us free from its power, thus allowing God to write His law on our hearts and show Himself in power as our God. He can then by His Spirit reveal to us His deepest truths—the deep mystery of Himself and His love. This redemption is meant to be our daily life and our eternal portion.

Here we now have the divine summary of our New Covenant inheritance. The last-named blessing, the pardon of sin, is the first in order, the root of all. The second, having God as our God, and the third, the divine teaching, are the fruit. The tree itself that grows on this root, and bears such fruit, is what is named first—the law in the heart.*

---

* On The Law Written on the Heart, see Note B, page 134.

The central demand of the Old Covenant—"Obey My voice, and I will be your God"—has now been met. With the law written on the heart, He can be our God and we shall be His people. Perfect harmony with God's will, holiness in heart and life, is the only thing that can satisfy God's heart or ours. And it is this the New Covenant gives in divine power: "*I will give them a heart* to know Me . . . and they will be My people, and I will be their God, for they will return to Me *with their whole heart*" (Jer. 24:7). It is on the condition of the heart, the new heart as *given by God*, that the New Covenant life hinges.

But if all this is meant to be literally and exactly true of God's people, why do we experience so little of this life in ourselves? There is but one answer: Because of our unbelief! We have spoken of the relationship between God and man in creation as that which the New Covenant is meant to make possible and real. But God will not compel. He can fulfill His purpose only as the heart is willing and accepts His offer. In the New Covenant all is by faith. Let us turn away from what human wisdom and human experience may say and ask God Himself to teach us what His Covenant means. If we persevere in this prayer in a humble and teachable spirit, we can most certainly count on its promise: "They will not teach again, each man his neighbor . . . saying, 'Know the Lord,' for they will all know Me." The teaching of God Himself, by the Holy Spirit, to make us understand what He says to us in His Word, is our Covenant right. Let us count upon it. It is only by a God-given faith that we can appropriate these God-given promises. And it is only by a God-given teaching and inward illumination that can we understand their meaning so as to believe them. When God teaches us the meaning of His promises in a heart yielded to His Holy Spirit, then alone we can believe and receive them in a power which makes them a reality in our life.

But is it really possible, amid the stress and strain of daily life, to walk in the experience of these blessings? Are they really meant for all God's children? Let us ask the question: Is it possible for God to do what He has promised? One part of the promise we believe—the complete and perfect pardon of sin. Why should we not believe the other part—the law written on the heart, and the divine fellowship and teaching? We have been so accustomed to separate what God has joined together—the objective, outward work of His Son, and the subjective, inward work of His Spirit—that we consider the glory of the New Covenant above the Old to consist chiefly in the redeeming work of Christ for us and not equally in the sanctifying work of the Spirit in us. It is because of this ignorance and unbelief in the indwelling of the Holy Spirit as the power through whom God fulfills the New Covenant promises that we come to not expect them to be made true in us.

Let us turn our hearts away from all past experience of failure, *as caused by nothing but unbelief*; let us admit fully and heartily what failure has taught us—the absolute impossibility of even a regenerate person walking in God's law in his own strength—and then turn our hearts quietly and trustfully to our own Covenant God. Let us hear what He says He will do for us and believe Him; let us rest on His unchangeable faithfulness and the surety of the Covenant, on His almighty power and the Holy Spirit working in us; and let us yield ourselves to Him as our God. He will prove that what He has done for us in Christ is not one bit more wonderful than what He will do in us every day by the Spirit of Christ.

Chapter

5

The Two Covenants –
In Christian Experience

"These two women are two covenants: one proceeding from Mount Sinai bearing children who are to be slaves; she is Hagar. Now this Hagar is Mount Sinai in Arabia and corresponds to the present Jerusalem, for she is in slavery with her children. But the Jerusalem above is free; she is our mother. . . . So then, brethren, we are not children of a bondwoman, but of the free woman. It was for freedom that Christ set us free; therefore keep standing firm and do not be subject again to a yoke of slavery."—Gal. 4:24–5:1.

THE HOUSE of Abraham was the Church of God of that age. The division in his house—one son born according to the flesh, the other according to the promise—was a divinely, ordained manifestation of the division there would be in all ages between the children of the bondwoman, those who serve God in the spirit of bondage, and the children of the free woman, those who serve Him in the Spirit of His Son. The passage teaches us what the whole epistle confirms: that the Galatians had become subject to a yoke of bondage and were not standing fast in the freedom which Christ has provided. Instead of living in the New Covenant, in the Jerusalem that is from above, in the liberty which the Holy Spirit gives, their whole walk proved that, though Christians, they were of the Old Covenant which brings forth children who are slaves. The passage teaches us the great truth, which it is of the utmost consequences for us to comprehend, that a man with a measure of knowledge and experience of the grace of God may prove, by a legal spirit, that he is yet under the Old Covenant to a large extent. And it will show us, with wonderful clearness, what the proofs are of the absence of true New Covenant life.

A careful study of the epistle shows us that the difference between the two Covenants is seen in three areas. The law with its works is contrasted to the hearing of faith, the flesh and its religion to the flesh crucified, the inability to do good to a walk in the liberty and power of the Spirit. May the Holy Spirit reveal to us this twofold life.

The first antithesis we find in Paul's words, "Did you receive the Spirit by the works of the law, or by hearing with faith?" (3:2). These Galatians had indeed been born into the New Covenant—they had received the Holy Spirit. But they had been led astray by Jewish teachers, and, though they had been justified by faith, they were seeking to be sanctified by works; for the maintenance and the growth of their Christian life they were looking to the observance of the law. They had not understood that, just as faith was the sole means to God's grace in the beginning, so also progress in the divine life is alone by faith, day by day receiving its strength from Christ alone—that in Jesus Christ nothing avails but faith working by love.

Almost every believer makes the same mistake as the Galatian Christians. Very few learn at conversion that it is only by faith

that we stand and walk and live. They have no understanding
of Paul's teaching about being dead to the law, freed from the
law—about the freedom with which Christ makes us free. "But
if you are led by the Spirit, you are not under the law" (5:18).
Regarding the law as a divine ordinance for our direction, they
consider themselves prepared by conversion to take up the fulfillment of the law as a natural duty. They do not know that in
the New Covenant the law written on the heart needs an unceasing faith in a divine power to enable us by that power to
keep it. They cannot understand that it is not to the law but to
a living Person that we are now bound, and that our obedience
and holiness are possible only by unceasing faith in His power
ever working in us. It is only when this is seen that we are truly
prepared to live in the New Covenant.

The second word that reveals the spirit of the Old Covenant is the word "flesh." Its contrast is the flesh crucified. Paul
asks: "Are you so foolish? Having begun by the Spirit, are you
now being perfected by the flesh?" (3:3). Flesh means our sinful human nature. At conversation the Christian has generally
no conception of the terrible evil of his self-life and the subtlety
with which it offers itself to take part in the service of God. It
may be most willing and diligent in God's service for a time; it
may devise numberless observances for making His worship
pleasing and attractive; and yet all this may be only what Paul
calls "making a good showing in the flesh," "glorying in the
flesh," in man's will and man's efforts. This power of the religious flesh is one of the great marks of the Old Covenant religion; it misses the deep humility and spirituality of the true
worship of God—a heart and life entirely dependent upon Him.

The proof that our religion is very much that of the religious flesh is that the sinful flesh will be found to flourish along

with it. It was thus with the Galatians. While they were making a good showing in the flesh and glorying in it, their daily life was full of bitterness, envy, hatred, and other sins. They were biting and devouring one another. Religious flesh and sinful flesh are one: no wonder that with a great deal of religion, temper and selfishness and worldliness are so often found side by side. The religion of the flesh cannot conquer sin.

What a contrast to the religion of the New Covenant! What place does the flesh have there? "Those who belong to Christ Jesus have *crucified the flesh* with its passions and desires" (5:24). Scripture speaks of the will of the flesh, the mind of the flesh, the desires of the flesh; all this the true believer has seen to be condemned and crucified in Christ—he has given it over to death. He not only accepts the cross (with its bearing of the curse and its redemption from it) as his entrance into life, but he glories in it as his only power day by day to overcome the flesh and the world. "I am crucified with Christ." "May it never be that I would boast, except in the cross of our Lord Jesus Christ, through which the world has been crucified to me, and I to the world" (6:14). Even as nothing less than the death of Christ was needed to inaugurate the New Covenant and the resurrection life that empowers it, so there is no entrance into the true New Covenant life other than by a partaking of that death.

"Fallen from grace" (5:4). This is a third word that describes the condition of these Galatians in their bondage in which they were unable to accomplish all true good. Paul is not speaking of a final falling away here, for he still addresses them as Christians, but of their having wandered from that walk in the way of enabling and sanctifying grace by which a Christian can get the victory over sin. As long as grace is principally connected with pardon and the entrance to the Christian life, the flesh is the only power in which to serve and work. But when we know what exceeding abundance of grace has been provided and how God "makes all grace abound, that we may have an abundance for every good deed," we know that as it is by faith so too it is by grace alone that we stand a single moment or take a single step.

The contrast to the life of spiritual impotence and failure is found in the words "the Spirit." "If you are led by the Spirit, you are not under the law" (5:18) with its demand on your own strength. "Walk by the Spirit, and you will not"—a definite, certain promise—"you will not carry out the desire of the flesh" (5:16). The Spirit gives liberty from the law, from the flesh, and from sin. "The fruit of the Spirit is love, joy, peace" (5:22). Of the New Covenant promise, "I will put *My Spirit* within you and *cause* you to walk in My statutes, and *you will be careful to observe* My ordinances" (Ezek. 36:27), the Spirit is the center and the sum. He is the power of the supernatural life of true obedience and holiness.

And what would have been the course that the Galatians would have taken if they had accepted this teaching of St. Paul? As they heard his question, "Now that you have come to know God . . . how is it that you turn back again to the weak and worthless elemental things, to which you desire to be enslaved all over again?" (4:9) they would have felt that there was but one course. Nothing could help them but at once to turn back to the path they had left. At the point where they had left it, they could enter again. With any one of them who wished to do so, this turning away from the Old Covenant legal spirit and the renewed surrender to the Mediator of the New Covenant could be the act of a moment—one single step. As the light of the New Covenant promise dawned on him and he saw how Christ was to be all, and faith all, and the Holy Spirit in the heart all, and the faithfulness of a Covenant-keeping God all in all, he would feel that he had but one thing to do—in utter weakness to yield himself to God, and in simple faith to count on Him to perform what He had spoken.

In Christian experience there may be still the Old Covenant life of enslavement and failure. In Christian experience there may be a life that gives way entirely to the New Covenant grace and spirit. In Christian experience, when the true vision has been received of what the New Covenant means, a faith that rests fully on the Mediator of the New Covenant can enter at once into the life which the Covenant secures.

I earnestly urge all believers who long to know to the utmost what the grace of God can work in them to carefully study this matter: whether or not our being in Old Covenant bondage is the reason for our failure, and whether a clear insight into the possibility of an entire change in our relationship to God is not what is needed to give us the help we seek. It may be we are seeking spiritual growth through a more diligent use of the means of grace and a more earnest striving to live in accordance with God's will, and yet we *entirely fail*. The reason is that there is a hidden root of evil that must be removed. That root is the spirit of bondage, the legal spirit of self-effort. This spirit hinders the humble faith that knows that God will work all and then yields to Him to accomplish it. This spirit may be found amidst very great zeal for God's service and very earnest prayer for His grace; it does not enjoy the rest of faith, and cannot overcome sin because it does not stand in the liberty with which Christ has made us free and does not know that where the Spirit of the Lord is there is liberty. There the soul can say: "The law of the

Spirit of life in Christ Jesus *has set me free* from the law of sin and of death" (Rom. 8:2). When once we admit heartily not only that there are failings in our life but also that there is something radically wrong that can be changed, we shall turn with a new interest, with a deeper confession of ignorance and inability, and with a hope that looks *to God alone* for teaching and strength, to find that in the New Covenant there is an actual provision for every need.

Chapter

6

The Everlasting Covenant

"They shall be My people, and I will be their God. . . . I will make an everlasting covenant with them that I will not turn away from them, to do them good; and I will put the fear of Me in their hearts so that they will not turn away from Me."—Jer. 32:38, 40.

"Moreover, I will give you a new heart and put a new spirit within you; and I will remove the heart of stone from your flesh and give you a heart of flesh. I will put my Spirit within you and cause you to walk in My statutes, and you will be careful to observe My ordinances. . . . I will make a covenant of peace with them; it will be an everlasting covenant with them."—Ezek. 36:26–27; 37:26.

W E HAVE had the words of the institution of the New Covenant. Let us listen to the further teaching we have concerning it in Jeremiah and Ezekiel, where God speaks of it as an everlasting Covenant.

In every covenant there are two parties. And the very foundation of a covenant rests on the thought that each party is to be faithful to the part he or she has undertaken to perform.

Unfaithfulness on either side breaks the covenant.

It was thus with the Old Covenant. God had said to Israel, *"Obey My voice, and I will be your God"* (Jer. 7:23, 11:4). These simple words contained the whole Covenant. And when Israel disobeyed, the Covenant was broken. The question of Israel's being able or not to obey was not taken into consideration: disobedience forfeited the privileges of the Covenant.

If a New Covenant were to be made and was to be better than the Old, one thing needed to be provided for. No New Covenant could be of any profit unless provision was made for securing obedience. Obedience there must be. God as Creator could never take His creatures into His favor and fellowship unless they obeyed Him. The thing would have been an impossibility. If the New Covenant is to be better than the Old—if it is to be an everlasting Covenant, never to be broken—it must make some sufficient provision for securing the obedience of the Covenant people.

And this is indeed the glory of the New Covenant, the glory that excels—that this provision has been made. In a way that no human thought could have devised, by a stipulation that never entered into any human covenant, by an undertaking in which God's infinite condescension and power and faithfulness are to be most wonderfully exhibited, by a supernatural mystery of divine wisdom and grace, the New Covenant provides a guarantee, not only for God's faithfulness, *but for man's too!* God Himself undertook to secure man's part as well as His own. It is crucial to understand this.

It is because this essential part of the New Covenant so exceeds and confounds all human thoughts of what a covenant means that Christians, from the Galatians downwards, have not been able to see and believe what the New Covenant really brings. They have thought that human unfaithfulness is a factor permanently to be reckoned with as something utterly unconquerable and incurable, and that the possibility of a life of obedience with the witness from within of a good conscience and from above of God's pleasure is not to be expected. They have, therefore, sought to stimulate the mind to its utmost by arguments and right motives, and have never realized that the Holy Spirit is to be the unceasing, universal, all-sufficient worker of everything that has to be wrought by the Christian.

Let us seek God earnestly that He would reveal to us by the Holy Spirit the things that He has prepared for those who love Him, things that the human heart has not conceived—the wonderful life of the New Covenant. It all depends upon our understanding of what God will work in us. Listen to what God says in Jeremiah 32:40 regarding the two parts of this everlasting Covenant, words given shortly after He had announced the New Covenant and in further clarification of it. The central thought of the Covenant, *that the heart is to be put right*, is here reiterated and confirmed. First: "I will make an everlasting covenant with them that *I will not turn away from them, to do them good.*" That is, God will be unchangeably faithful. He will not turn from being good to us. "And I will put the fear of Me in their hearts *so that they will not turn away from Me.*" This promise is the second half: Israel will be unchangeably faithful too. And that is because God will inspire them to fear Him so that they will never turn away from Him. *Just as little as God will turn from them will they turn away from Him!* As faithfully as He undertakes for the fulfillment of His part will He undertake for the fulfillment of *their* part, so that they will not depart from Him!

Listen now to God's word in Ezekiel in regard to one of the

terms of His Covenant of peace, His everlasting Covenant: "I will put My spirit within you and *cause you to walk in My statutes, and you will be careful to observe My ordinances*" (Ezek. 36:27). In the Old Covenant we have nothing of this sort. We have, on the contrary, from the story of the golden calf and the breaking of the tablets of the Covenant onward, the sad fact of continual departure from God. We find God longing for what He would so have desired to see, but it was not to be found. "Oh, that they had such a heart in them, that they would fear Me and keep all My commandments always" (Deut. 5:29). We find throughout the book of Deuteronomy a thing without parallel in the history of any religion or religious lawgiver— that Moses most distinctly prophesies their forsaking of God, with the terrible curses and dispersion that would come upon them. It is only at the close of his threatenings (Deut. 30:6–8) that he gives the promise of the new time that would come: "The Lord your God will circumcise your heart and the heart of your descendants, to love the Lord your God with all your heart and with all your soul, . . . and *you shall obey* the Lord."

The whole Old Covenant was dependent on man's faithfulness: "The Lord your God *keeps His covenant* with those *who keep His commandments.*" God's keeping the Covenant availed little if man did not keep it. Nothing could help man until the "*if you will diligently keep*" of the law was replaced by the word of promise, "I will put My Spirit within you . . . and *you will be careful to observe* My ordinances." The one supreme difference of the New Covenant—the one thing for which the Mediator and the blood and the Spirit were given, the one fruit God sought and committed Himself to bring forth—was this: a heart filled with both the fear and love of God, a heart in which His Spirit and His law dwells, a heart that delights to do His will.

Here is the inmost secret of the New Covenant. It deals with the heart of man in a way that involves divine power. It not only appeals to the heart by every motive of fear or love, of duty or gratitude—that the law also did—but it reveals God Himself, cleansing our heart and making it new, changing it entirely from a heart of stone into a heart of flesh—a tender, living, loving heart. It includes putting His Spirit within it and thus, by His almighty power and love breathing and working in it, making the promise true: "*I will cause you to* walk in My statutes, and *you will be careful to observe* My ordinances." A heart in perfect harmony with God, a life and walk in His way— God has pledged in covenant to work this in us. He undertakes for our part in the Covenant as much as for His own.

This is nothing less than the restoration of the original relationship between God and the man He had made in His likeness. He was on earth to be the very image of God because God was to live and to work all in him; and he was to find his glory and blessedness in thus owing all to God. This is now the exceeding glory of the New Covenant, of the Pentecostal dispensation, that by the Holy Spirit God could again be the indwelling life of His people and so make the promise a reality: "I will cause you to walk in My statutes."

With God's presence secured to us every moment of the day ("I will not turn away from them"); with God's "fear put into our heart" by His own Spirit, and our heart thus responding to His holy presence; with our hearts thus made right with God—we can, we shall walk in His statutes and keep His ordinances.

The great sin of Israel under the Old Covenant—that by which they greatly grieved Him—was this: they limited the Holy One of Israel. Under the New Covenant there is no less danger

of this sin. *It makes it impossible for God to fulfill His promises.*
Let us seek, above everything, for the Holy Spirit's teaching
that will show us exactly what God has established the New
Covenant for, that we may honor Him by believing all that His
love has prepared for us.

And if we ask for the cause of the unbelief that prevents the
fulfillment of the promise, we shall find that it is not far to
seek. It is, in most cases, a lack of desire for the promised blessing. Think of those who came to Jesus on earth: the intensity of
their desire for the healing they needed made them ready and
glad to believe His word. Where God's law has done its full
work so that the desire to be freed from sin is strong and mas-
ters the heart, the promise of the New Covenant, when really
understood, comes like bread to a starving man. The subtle
unbelief that thinks it impossible to be kept from sinning, however, cuts away the power of accepting the provision of the everlasting Covenant. God's Word, "I will put the fear of Me in
their hearts so that *they will not* turn away from Me. . . . I will
put My Spirit within you and *you will* be careful to observe My
ordinances," is so often understood only in some feeble sense,
according to our experience. And so the soul settles down into
a despair or a self-contentment that says it can never be otherwise.

Let me say to every reader who desires to be able to fully
believe all that God says: Cherish every whisper of the conscience and of the Spirit that convinces of sin. Whatever it might
be—a hasty temper, a sharp word, an unloving or impatient
thought, anything of selfishness or self-will—cherish that which
condemns it in you as part of the schooling that is to bring you
to Christ and the full possession of His salvation. The New
Covenant is meant to meet the need for a power of not sinning,

a power which the Old could not give. Come with that need; it will prepare and open the heart for all the everlasting Covenant secures for you. It will bring you to that humble and entire dependence upon God in His omnipotence and His faithfulness in which He *can* and *will* work all He has promised.

Chapter

7

———

The New Covenant:
A Ministry of the Spirit

*"You are a letter of Christ, cared for by us, written not
with ink but with the Spirit of the living God, not on tablets
of stone but on tablets of human hearts. . . . Our adequacy is
from God who also made us adequate as servants of a new
covenant, not of the letter but of the Spirit; for the letter kills,
but the Spirit gives life. But if the ministry of death . . . came
with glory, . . . how will the ministry of the Spirit fail to be
even more with glory? For if the ministry of condemnation has
glory, much more does the ministry of righteousness abound
in glory."*—2 Cor. 3:3, 5–9.

I N THIS wonderful chapter
Paul reminds the Corinthians, in speaking of his ministry among
them, of what its chief characteristics were. As a ministry of the
New Covenant he contrasts it, and the whole dispensation of
which it is a part, with that of the Old. The Old was graven on
stone, the New on the heart. The Old could be written in ink
and was distinguished by the letter that kills; the New is distinguished by the Spirit who makes alive. The Old was a ministry

of condemnation and death; the New, of righteousness and life. The Old indeed had its glory, for it was by divine appointment and brought its divine blessing; but it was a glory that was to fade away, and had no glory in comparison to the much greater glory of that which lasts. With the Old, there was the veil on the heart; in the New, the veil is taken away from the face and the heart, for in it the Spirit of the Lord gives liberty. And we, who with unveiled faces all reflect the Lord's glory, are being transformed with ever-increasing glory into His image, by the Spirit of the Lord. This glory that excels proves its power in this, that it not only characterizes the dispensation on its divine side but also so exerts its power in the heart and life of its subjects that it is seen in them also.

Think a moment about the contrast. The Old Covenant functioned as the letter that kills. The law came with its literal instruction and sought by the knowledge it gave of God's will to appeal to man's fear and his love—to his natural powers of mind and conscience and will. It spoke to him as if he could obey so that it might convince him of what he did not know, the fact that he could not obey. And so it fulfilled its mission: "This commandment, which was to result in life, proved to result in death for me" (Rom. 7:10). In the New, on the contrary, how different everything is. Instead of the compelling "letter" there is the Spirit who gives life, who breathes the very life of God, the life of heaven into us. Instead of a law graven on stone, the law is written on the heart—worked into the heart's affection and powers, making it one with them. Instead of a vain attempt to work from the outside inward, the Spirit and the law are put into the inward parts to work outward in life and walk.

This passage brings into view the distinctive blessing of the

New Covenant. In working out our salvation God bestowed upon us two wonderful gifts. We read: "*God sent forth His Son . . .* so that He might redeem those who were under the law, that we might receive the adoption as sons. Because you are sons, *God has sent forth the Spirit of His Son* into our hearts, crying, 'Abba! Father!'" (Gal. 4:4–6). Here we have the two parts of God's work in salvation. The one, the more objective, is what He did that we might *become* His children: He sent forth His Son. The second, the more subjective, is what He did that we might *live like* His children: He has sent forth the Spirit of His Son into our hearts. In the former, we have the external manifestation of the work of redemption; in the other, its inward appropriation. The former was for the sake of the latter. These two halves form one great whole and may not be separated.

In the promises of the New Covenant, as we find them in Jeremiah and Ezekiel as well as in our text and many other passages of Scripture, it is clear that God's great object in salvation is to get possession of the heart. The heart is the *real* life; with the heart a man loves and wills and acts. The heart *makes* the man. God created man's heart for His own dwelling place so that in it He might reveal His love and His glory. Then God sent Christ to accomplish a redemption by which man's heart could be won back to Him, for nothing but that could satisfy God. And *that* is what is accomplished when the Holy Spirit makes the heart of God's child what it should be. The whole work of Christ's redemption—His atonement and victory, His exaltation and intercession, His glory at the right hand of God—are only preparatory to what is the chief triumph of His grace: the renewal of the heart to be the temple of God. Through Christ God gives the Holy Spirit to glorify Him in the heart by working there all that He has done and is doing for the soul.

Some religious teachers seem to fear that by giving promi-
nence to Christ's work in the believer's heart by the Holy Spirit
they might detract from Christ's work on the cross or His work
now in heaven. The result has been that the indwelling of the
Holy Spirit and His mighty work as *the life of the heart* are little
known by many. But if we look carefully at what the New Covenant promises really mean, we shall see how the "sending forth
the Spirit of His Son into our hearts" is indeed the consummation and crown of Christ's redeeming work. We need to consider what these promises imply.

In the Old Covenant man had failed in what he had to do;
in the New, God is to do everything in him. The Old could
only convict of sin; the New is to put it away and cleanse the
heart from its filthiness. In the Old it was the heart that was
wrong; for the New, a new heart is provided—into which God
puts His fear and His law and His love. The Old demanded,
but failed to secure obedience; in the New, *God* causes us to
walk in His ordinances. The New is to fit man for a true holiness, a true fulfillment of the law of loving God with the whole
heart and our neighbors as ourselves—a walk truly well-pleasing to God. The New transforms a man from glory to glory
after the image of Christ, all because the Spirit of God's Son is
given into the heart. The Old gave no power; in the New *all* is
by the Spirit, the mighty power of God. As complete as the
reign and power of Christ is on the throne of heaven, so is His
dominion on the throne of the heart by His Holy Spirit given
to us.*

It is as we bring all these traits of the New Covenant life

---

* See Note C, on George Müller, page 138.

together into one focus and look at the heart of God's child as the object of this mighty redemption that we shall begin to understand what is secured to us and what it is that we are to expect from our Covenant God. We shall see that the glory of the ministry of the Spirit is that God can fill our heart with His love and make it His dwelling place.

We are accustomed to say, and truly so, that the worth of the Son of God, who came to die for us, is the measure of the worth of the soul in God's sight and of the greatness of the work that had to be done to save it. Let us also see that the divine glory of the Holy Spirit, the Spirit of the Father and the Son, is the measure of God's longing to have our heart wholly for Himself. It is also the measure of the glory of the work that is to be accomplished in us, and of the power by which that work will be brought about.

We shall see that the glory of the ministry of the Spirit is none other than the glory of the Lord—as it is not only in heaven but presently resting upon us and dwelling in us, and changing us from one degree of glory to another. The inconceivable glory of our exalted Lord in heaven has its counterpart here on earth in the exceeding glory of the Holy Spirit who glorifies Him in us, who lays His glory on us as He changes us into His likeness.

The New Covenant has no power to save and to bless except as it is a ministry of the Spirit. That Spirit works in lesser or greater degree as He is neglected and grieved or yielded to and trusted. Let us honor Him and give Him His place as the Spirit of the New Covenant by accepting all He waits to do for us.

He is the great gift of the Covenant. His coming from heaven was proof that the Mediator of the Covenant was on the throne in glory and could now make us partakers of the heavenly life.

He is the only teacher of what the Covenant means because, dwelling in our heart, He awakens there the thought and the desire for what God has prepared for us.

He is the Spirit of faith, who enables us to believe the otherwise incomprehensible blessing and power in which the New Covenant works, and to claim it as our own.

He is the Spirit of grace and of power by whom obedience to the Covenant and fellowship with God can be maintained without interruption.

He Himself is the possessor and the bearer and the communicator of all the Covenant promises, the revealer and the glorifier of Jesus, its Mediator and guarantee.

To believe fully in the Holy Spirit as the present and abiding and all-comprehending gift of the New Covenant has been to many an entrance into its fullness of blessing.

Begin at once, child of God, to give the Holy Spirit the place in your life that He has in God's plan. Be still before God and believe that He is within you, and ask the Father to work in you through Him. Regard yourself, your spirit as well as your body, with holy reverence as His temple. Let the consciousness of His holy presence and working fill you with holy calm and fear. And be sure that all that God calls you to be, Christ through His Spirit will work in you.

Chapter

8

The Two Covenants:
The Transition

*"Now the God of peace, who brought up from the dead
the great Shepherd of the sheep through the blood of the eternal covenant, even Jesus our Lord, equip you in every good
thing to do His will, working in us that which is pleasing in
His sight, through Jesus Christ, to whom be the glory forever
and ever."*—Heb. 13:20–21.

THE TRANSITION from the
Old Covenant to the New was not slow or gradual but was
brought about by a tremendous crisis; nothing less than the
death of Christ was the close of the Old Covenant. Nothing
less that His resurrection from the dead, through the blood of
the eternal Covenant, was the opening of the New. The path of
preparation that led up to the crisis was long and slow, but the
rending of the veil, that symbolized the end of the old worship,
was the work of a moment. By a death once for all, Christ's
work as fulfiller of the law was forever finished. He brought the
law to its end. By a resurrection in the power of an endless life,

the Covenant of Life was ushered in.

These events have an infinite significance, for they reveal the character of the Covenants they are related to. The death of Christ shows the true nature of the Old Covenant. It is elsewhere called "a ministry of death" (2 Cor. 3:7). It brought forth nothing but death. It ended in death; yes, only by death could the life that had been lived under it be brought to an end. The New was to be a Covenant of Life; it had its birth in the omnipotent resurrection power that brought Christ up from the dead. Its one mark and blessing is that all it gives comes not only as a *promise* but as an *experience* in the power of an endless life. The death reveals the utter *inefficacy* and *insufficiency* of the Old; the life imparts to us forever all that the New has to offer. An insight into the completeness of the transition, as seen in Christ, prepares us for comprehending the reality of the change in our life, when, "as Christ was raised from the dead through the glory of the Father, so we too might walk in newness of life" (Rom. 6:4).

The complete difference between the life in the Old and the New is remarkably illustrated by a passage in Hebrews. After having said that a death for the redemption of transgressions had to take place before the New Covenant could be established, the writer adds, "Where a covenant is, there must of necessity be the death of the one who made it" (9:16). Before any heir can obtain his legacy, its first owner must have died. The old proprietorship, the old life, must disappear entirely before the new heir, the new life, can enter upon the inheritance. Nothing but death can work the transference of the property. It is even so with Christ, with the Old and the New Covenant life, with our own deliverance from the Old and our entrance into the New. Now, having been "made to die to the law through the body of Christ . . . we have been released from the law, having died to that by which we were bound"—here is the completeness of the deliverance from Christ's side—"so that we serve"—here is the completeness of the change in our experience—"in newness of the Spirit and not in oldness of the letter" (Rom. 7:4, 6).

The transition, if it is to be real and whole, must take place by a death. As with Christ, the Mediator of the Covenant, so it must be with His people, the heirs of the Covenant. In Him we are dead to sin; in Him we are dead to the law. Just as Adam died to God and from him we inherit a nature that is actually dead in sin, dead to God and His kingdom, so in Christ we died to sin and inherit a new nature that is actually dead to sin and its dominion. It is when the Holy Spirit reveals and makes real to us this death to sin and to the law as the one condition of a life to God that this transition from the Old to the New Covenant can be fully realized in us.

The Old was, and was meant to be, a "ministry of death"; until it has completely done its work in us there is no complete discharge from its power. The man who sees that self is incurably evil and must die, who gives self utterly to death as he sinks before God in utter impotence and in surrender to His working, who consents to death with Christ on the cross as what he deserves and in faith accepts it as his only deliverance— he alone is prepared to be led by the Holy Spirit into the full enjoyment of the New Covenant life. He will learn to understand how completely death makes an end to all self-effort, and how, as he lives in Christ to God, everything henceforth is to be the work of God Himself.

See how beautifully our text brings out this truth: that just as much as Christ's resurrection out of death was the work of

God Himself, so our spiritual life is equally to be wholly God's own work too. As real and as wonderful as Christ's transition from death to life was, so should be our experience of what the New Covenant life is to bring. Notice the subject of the two verses. In Hebrews 13:20 we have what God *has done* in raising Christ from the dead; in verse 21, what God *is to do in us*, working in us what is pleasing to Him. (20) "The God of peace, who brought up from the dead the great Shepherd of the sheep . . . even Jesus our Lord," (21) "equip you in every good thing to do His will, working in us that which is pleasing in His sight, through Jesus Christ." We have the name of our Lord Jesus twice. In the first case it refers to what God has done to Christ for us, raising Him; in the second, to what God is doing through Christ in us, working His pleasure in us. Because it is the same God continuing in us the work He began in Christ, it is in us just what it was in Christ. In Christ's death we see Him in utter submission allowing and counting on God to work all and give Him life. God accomplished the wonderful transition. In us we see the same; it is only as we give ourself unto that death too, as we entirely cease from self and its works, as we lie as in the grave waiting for God to work all, that the God of resurrection life can work in us all His good pleasure.

It was "through the blood of the eternal covenant," with its atonement for sin and its destruction of sin's power, that God effected that resurrection. It is through that same blood that we are redeemed and freed from the power of sin and made partakers of Christ's resurrection life. The more we study the New Covenant, the more we shall see that its one aim is to restore man from the Fall into the life in God for which he was created. It does this first by delivering him from the power of sin in Christ's death, and then by taking possession of his heart, his life, for God to work all in him by the Holy Spirit.

The whole argument of the Epistle to the Hebrews as to the Old and New Covenants is here summed up in these concluding verses. Just as He raised Christ from the dead, the God of the eternal Covenant can and will now equip you in every good thing to do His will, working in you that which is pleasing in His sight, through Jesus Christ. Your doing His will is the reason for creation and redemption. God's working it all in you is what redemption has made possible. The Old Covenant of law and effort and failure has ended in condemnation and death. The New Covenant is coming to give, in all whom the law has slain and brought to bow in their utter impotence, the law written on the heart, the Spirit dwelling there, and God working all, both to will and to do, through Jesus Christ.

Oh, for a divine revelation that the transition from Christ's death, in its impotence, to His life in God's power, is the image, the pledge, the power of our transition out of the Old Covenant, when it has slain us, to the New, with God working in us all in all!

The transition from Old to New as effected in Christ was sudden. Is it so in the believer? Not always. In us it depends upon a revelation. There have been cases in which a believer, sighing and struggling against the yoke of bondage, has in one moment been enabled to see what a complete salvation the New Covenant brings to the inner life through the ministry of the Spirit, and by faith he has entered at once into his rest. There have been other cases in which as gradual as the dawn of the day the light of God has risen upon the heart. God's offer of entrance into the enjoyment of our New Covenant privileges is always urgent and immediate. Every believer is a child of the New Covenant and heir of all its promises. The death of the

Covenant-maker gives him full right to immediate possession. God longs to bring us into the land of promise; let us not come short through unbelief.

There may be someone who is uncertain that such a mighty change in his life is within his reach, and yet he would like to know what he is to do if there is to be any hope of his attaining it. As I have just said, the death of any covenant-maker gives the heir immediate right to the inheritance. And yet the heir, if he is a minor, does not enter into the possession. A set number of years ends the stage of minority on earth and then he is no longer under guardians. But in the spiritual life the state of pupilage ends not at the expiration of years but at the moment the minor proves his fitness for being made free from the law—by accepting the liberty there is in Christ Jesus. The transition—as with the Old Covenant, as with Christ, as with the disciples—comes when the time is fulfilled and all things are now ready.

But what is one to do who is longing to be made ready? Acknowledge the sentence of death on everything that is of the self-life: take and keep the place before God of utter unworthiness and helplessness; sink down before Him in humility, meekness, patience, and resignation to His will and mercy. Fix your heart upon the great and mighty God who in His grace will work in you beyond what you can ask or think and will make you a monument of His mercy. Believe that every blessing of the Covenant of grace is yours; by Christ's death you are entitled to it all—and on that faith act, knowing that all is yours. The new heart is yours; the law written on the heart is yours; the Holy Spirit, the seal of the Covenant, is yours. Act on this faith, and count upon God as faithful and able to make true in you all the power and glory of His everlasting Covenant.

May God reveal to us the difference between the two lives under the Old and the New; the resurrection power of the New, with God working all in us; the power of the transition secured to us in death with Christ and life in Him. And may He teach us now to trust Christ Jesus for a full participation in all the New Covenant secures.

Chapter

9

The Blood of the Covenant

"Behold the blood of the covenant, which the Lord has made with you."—Ex. 24:8; Heb. 9:20.

"This cup is the new covenant in My blood."—1 Cor. 11:25; Matt. 26:28.

"The blood of the covenant by which he was sanctified."—Heb. 10:29.

"The blood of the eternal covenant."—Heb. 13:20.

THE BLOOD is one of the wisest, the deepest, the mightiest, and the most heavenly of the thoughts of God. It lies at the very root of both Covenants, but especially of the New Covenant. The difference between the two Covenants is the difference between the blood of beasts and the blood of the Lamb of God. The power of the New Covenant has no lesser measure than the worth of the blood of the Son of God! Our Christian experience ought to know of no standard for peace with God and purity from sin and power over the world but what the blood of Christ can give! If we would enter truly and fully into all that the New Covenant is meant to be to us, let us ask God to reveal to us the worth and the power of the blood of the Covenant, the precious blood of Christ.

The first Covenant was not initiated without blood. There could be no Covenant of friendship between a holy God and sinful, rebellious men without atonement and reconciliation, and no atonement without a death as the penalty of sin. God declared: "I have given you the blood on the altar to make atonement for your souls" (Lev. 17:11). The blood shed in death meant the death of a sacrifice slain for the sin of man; the blood sprinkled on the altar meant that vicarious death accepted by God for the sinful one. There was no forgiveness and no Covenant without blood-shedding.

All this was but a type and shadow of what was one day to become a mysterious reality. What no mere man or angel could have conceived—what even now surpasses all understanding—this Christ did: the eternal Son of God took flesh and blood, and then shed that blood as the blood of the New Covenant, not merely to ratify it but to open up the way to God and make reconciliation possible. Beyond any mortal's comprehension, Christ Jesus became the living power by which entrance into the Covenant was to be obtained and all life in it be secured. Until we form our expectation of a life in the New Covenant according to the inconceivable worth and power of the blood of God's Son, we will never catch a glimpse into the entirely supernatural and heavenly life that a child of God may live. Let us consider the threefold light in which Scripture teaches us to regard it.

In the passage from Hebrews 9:15 we read: "For this reason Christ is the Mediator of a new covenant, so that, since a death has taken place for the redemption of the transgressions that were committed under the first covenant, those who have been called may receive the promise of the eternal inheritance." The sins committed during the span of the first Covenant, which had only figuratively been atoned for, had accumulated before God. A death was needed for the redemption of these. In that death and blood-shedding of the Lamb of God, not only were these atoned for but the power of all sin was forever broken.

The blood of the New Covenant is redemption blood, a purchase price and ransom from the power of sin and the law. In any purchase made on earth the transference of property from the old owner to the new is complete. Its worth may be extremely great and one's attachment to it ever so strong, but if the price is paid it is gone forever from the person who owned it. The hold that sin had on us was terrible. No thought can comprehend its legitimate claim on us under God's law, its awful, tyrannical power in enslaving us. But the blood of God's Son has been paid. "You were not redeemed with perishable things like silver and gold from your futile way of life inherited from your forefathers, but with precious blood, as of a lamb unblemished and spotless, the blood of Christ" (1 Pet. 1:18 19). We have been rescued, ransomed, redeemed out of our old natural life under the power of sin—utterly and eternally. *Sin has not the slightest claim on us, nor the slightest power over us, unless it is given dominion through our ignorance or unbelief or halfheartedness.* Our New Covenant birthright is to stand in the freedom with which Christ has made us free. Until the soul sees and desires and accepts the redemption and the liberty for which the blood of the Son of God was the purchase price, and claims its completeness and its security, it never can fully live the New Covenant life.

As wonderful as the *blood-shedding* is for our redemption so is the *blood-sprinkling* for our cleansing. Here is another of the spiritual mysteries of the New Covenant which lose their power when understood merely by human wisdom, without the ministry of the Spirit of life. When Scripture speaks of "having our hearts sprinkled clean from an evil conscience" (Heb. 10:22) and of "the blood of Christ cleansing our conscience" (Heb. 9:14), or refers to our singing here on earth "to Him who released us from our sins by His blood" (Rev. 1:5), it brings this mighty, quickening blood of the Lamb into direct contact with our hearts. It gives the assurance that that blood in its infinite worth, in its divine sin-cleansing power, can keep us clean in our walk in the sight and the light of God. It is as this blood of the New Covenant is known and trusted and waited for, and received from God through the Spirit's mighty operation in the heart, that we shall begin to believe that the blessed promise of a New Covenant life and walk can be fulfilled.

There is another aspect that Scripture teaches concerning this blood of the New Covenant. When the Jews contrasted Moses with our Lord Jesus, He said: "Unless you eat the flesh of the Son of Man and drink His blood, you have no life in yourselves. . . . He who eats My flesh and drinks My blood abides in Me, and I in him" (John 6:53–56). As if the redeeming and sprinkling and washing and sanctifying does not sufficiently express the intense inwardness of its action and its power to permeate our whole being, the drinking of this precious blood is declared to be indispensable to having spiritual life. If we would enter deep into the spirit and power of the New Covenant, let us, by the Holy Spirit, drink deep of this cup—the cup of the New Covenant in Christ's blood.

On account of sin there could be no covenant between man and God without blood. And no New Covenant could commence without the shed blood of the Son of God. As the cleansing away of sins was the first condition in making a covenant, so it is equally the first condition for an entrance into it. It has always been found that a deeper appropriation of the blessings of the Covenant must be preceded by a new and deeper cleansing from sin. In Ezekiel the words about God's causing us to walk in His statutes are preceded by "*I will cleanse you from all your filthiness*" (36:25). And then later we read (37:23, 26), "They will no longer defile themselves . . . with any of their transgressions . . . *but I will cleanse them*. And they will be My people, and I will be their God. . . . I will make a covenant of peace with them; it will be an everlasting covenant with them." The confession and casting away and the cleansing away of sin in the blood are the indispensable, and all-sufficient, preparation for a life in everlasting covenant with God.

Many feel that they do not understand or realize this wonderful power of the blood. Meditating on it does not help them; even prayer does not appear to bring the light they seek. Truly, the blood of Christ is a divine mystery and surpasses all thought. Like every spiritual and heavenly blessing, it needs to be imparted to us by the Holy Spirit. It was "through the eternal Spirit" that Christ offered the sacrifice in which the blood was shed. The blood had the life of Christ, the life empowered by the Spirit, in it. The outpouring of the blood for us was to prepare the way for the outpouring of the Spirit on us. It is the Holy Spirit, and He alone, who can minister the blood of the everlasting Covenant in power.

Just as the Holy Spirit leads the soul to its initial faith in the pardon Christ's blood has purchased and the peace it gives, He leads further to the knowledge and experience of its cleansing power. Here again, by faith—faith in an operation of God's mighty power—a cleansing is effected that gives a clean heart.

This clean heart is first known and accepted by faith, apart from signs or feelings, apart from sense or reason, and then experienced in the joy and the fellowship with God it brings. Oh, to believe in the blood of the everlasting Covenant and the cleansing that the Holy Spirit ministers!

Let us believe in the ministry of the Holy Spirit until our whole life in the New Covenant becomes entirely His work, to the glory of the Father and of Christ!

The blood of the Covenant—oh, mystery of mysteries! Oh, grace above all grace! Oh, the mighty power of God, opening the way into the Holiest and into our hearts and into the New Covenant, where the Holy One and our heart meet! Let us ask God earnestly, by His Holy Spirit, to make us know what it is and what it works. This transition from the death of the Old Covenant to the life of the New is "through the blood of the eternal Covenant." And it is for us.

Chapter

10

Jesus, the Mediator of the New Covenant

"I will appoint You as a covenant to the people."—Isa. 42:6; 49:8.

"The Lord . . . will suddenly come to His temple; and the messenger of the covenant, in whom you delight, behold, He is coming."—Mal. 3:1.

"Jesus has become the guarantee of a better covenant." —Heb 7:22.

"The mediator of a better covenant, which has been enacted on better promises. . . . The mediator of a new covenant. . . . You have come . . . to Jesus, the mediator of a new covenant." —Heb. 8:6; 9:15; 12:22–24.

WE HAVE here four titles given to our Lord Jesus in connection with the New Covenant.

First, He Himself is called a *Covenant*. This makes sense because the union between God and man, which the Covenant aims at, was accomplished in Him personally; because in Him the reconciliation between the human and the divine was perfectly effected; because in Him His people find the Covenant with all its blessings. He is all that God has to give and so provides us assurance that it is given.

Second, He is called the *Messenger* of the Covenant because He came to establish and to *proclaim* it.

Third, He, is the *Guarantee* and the *Guarantor* of the Covenant—not only because He paid our debt, but because He is both our guarantee that God will fulfill *His* part and God's guarantor that we will fulfill *our* part.

And fourth, He is *Mediator* of the Covenant because, as the Covenant was established in His atoning blood, is administered and applied by Him, is entered upon alone by faith in Him, so it is known *experientially* only through the power of His resurrection life and His never-ceasing intercession.

All these names point to this one truth: *In the New Covenant Christ is all in all.*

The subject is so large that it would be impossible to enter upon all the various aspects of this precious truth. Christ's work in atonement and intercession, in His bestowal of pardon and of the Holy Spirit, in His daily communication of grace and strength—these are truths that lie at the very foundation of the faith of Christians. We need not speak more of them here. What does need to be made clear to many, however, is how by faith in Christ as the Mediator of the New Covenant we actually have access to the enjoyment of all its promised blessings. We have already seen in our study of the New Covenant how all these blessings culminate in one thing—that the heart of man is to be made right as the only possible way of his living in favor with God and of God's love finding its satisfaction in him. He is to receive a heart to reverence God, to love God with all his being, to obey God and keep all His statutes. All that Christ did and does has this for its aim, and all the higher blessings of peace and fellowship flow from this. In this Covenant God's saving power and love find the highest proof of their triumph over sin. Nothing so reveals the grace of God, the power of Jesus Christ, the reality of salvation, the blessedness of the New Covenant, as the heart of a believer where sin once abounded but where grace now abounds more exceedingly within it.

I do not know how I can better set forth the glory of our blessed Lord Jesus as He accomplishes the object of His redeeming work and takes entire possession of the human heart than by pointing out the place He takes and the work He does in the case of a person who is being led out of Old Covenant bondage into the experience of the promise and power of the New Covenant.* In studying the work of the Mediator in an individual we may get a truer concept of the real glory and greatness of the work He actually accomplishes than if we only think of the work He has done for us all.

Let us see how entrance into the New Covenant blessing is attained.

The first step toward it is the believer's sense of sin. He sees that the New Covenant promises do not seem to be true in his experience. There is not only indwelling sin, but he finds that he gives way to anger, self-will, worldliness, and other known violations of God's law. The obedience to which God calls him is not his, and so his conscience condemns him. It is through this conviction of sin that a desire for the full New Covenant blessing must have its rise. Where, however, there is the assumption that obedience is an impossibility and that nothing but a life of failure is to be expected, it is useless to speak of

---

* For a practical illustration in the life of Canon Battersby, see note D on page 144.

God's promise or power. The heart cannot respond when it is sure that the liberty spoken of is a dream. But where the dissatisfaction with one's state has wrought a longing for something better, the heart is open to receive the message.

Now comes the second step. As the person's mind is directed to the literal meaning of the terms of the New Covenant with its promises of cleansing from sin, of a heart filled with reverence for God's law, and of power to keep God's commands and never to depart from Him, the longing begins to grow into a hope. As the believer's eye is fixed on Jesus the Guarantor of the Covenant, who will Himself make it all true—and as the voice is heard of witnesses who can declare how, after years of bondage, all this has been fulfilled in them—the inquiry is made as to what is needed to enter this blessed life.

Then follows the third step. The heart-searching question comes as to whether we are willing to give up every evil habit, all our own self-will, all that is of the spirit of the world, and surrender ourselves to be wholly and exclusively for Jesus. God cannot take complete possession of a person and bless him wonderfully and work in him mightily unless He has him completely, yea, wholly for Himself. Happy is the Christian who is ready for any sacrifice.

Now comes the last, the simplest, and yet often the most difficult step. And here it is a person needs to know Jesus as Mediator of the Covenant. As we hear of the life of holiness and victory over sin that the Covenant promises, and hear that it will be to us according to our faith—so that if we claim it in faith it will surely be ours—the heart often fails for fear. I am willing, but have I the power to make and maintain this full surrender? Have I the power, the strong faith, to grasp and hold this offered blessing so that it will become and continue to be mine? How such questions perplex the soul—until it finds the answer to them in the one word *Jesus*! It is He who will bestow the power to make the surrender and to believe.

Reader, this is as surely and as exclusively Christ's work as atonement and continual intercession are His alone. As sure as it was His to win and ascend the throne, it is His to prove His dominion in the individual soul. It is He, the Living One, who has divine power to work and maintain the life of communion and victory within us. He is the Mediator and Guarantor of the Covenant—He, the God-man, who has undertaken not only for all that God requires but for all that we need too.

When this is seen, the believer learns that here, just as at conversion, it is all by faith. The one thing needed now is to turn from self and anything it could or need do—to let go of self and fall into the arms of Jesus. He is the Mediator of the New Covenant: it is His privilege and duty to lead us into it. In the assurance that Jesus and every New Covenant blessing is already ours by virtue of our being God's children, and with the desire now to appropriate and enjoy what we have hitherto allowed to lie unused, let us surrender. Let us claim and accept our heritage as a present possession. I urge you: dare boldly to take the heavenly gift—a life in Christ according to the better promises. By faith receive Jesus as your personal Mediator of the New Covenant, one who ministers both in heaven and in your heart. He is the Mediator who makes effectual the Covenant between the Father and you.

The fear has sometimes been expressed that if we stress the work that Christ does in the believer's heart, we may be drawn away from trusting in what He did once on the cross. The answer is simple. It is *with the heart alone* that Christ can be truly known or honored. It is *in the heart* that the work of grace is to be done and the saving power of Christ is to be displayed. It is primarily *in the heart* that the Holy Spirit has His sphere of work. He is to work Christ's likeness *there*; it is *there* He can best glorify Christ. The Spirit can glorify Christ daily by revealing His saving power *in us.*

If we were to speak of what *we are to do* in cleansing our heart and keeping it right, the fear would be well-grounded. But the New Covenant calls us to the very opposite. What it tells us about the atonement and the righteousness of God that Jesus won for us will be our only glory even amidst the highest holiness of heaven. Christ's work of holiness here in the heart can only deepen consciousness of His righteousness as our only plea. The sanctifying work of the Spirit, as the fulfillment of the New Covenant promises, is simply His taking of the things of Christ and revealing and imparting them to us. The deeper our entrance into the New Covenant gift of a new heart, the fuller will be our knowledge and our love of Him who is the Mediator. The Covenant deals with the *heart*—that Christ may *dwell there by faith.* As we look at the heart—not in the light of feeling or experience but in the light of faith in God's Covenant—we shall come to realize, as God does, that there Christ manifests Himself and there He and the Father come to make their abode.

Chapter

11

Jesus, the Guarantor
of a Better Covenant

*"And inasmuch of it was not without an oath . . . so much
the more Jesus has become the guarantee of a better covenant.
. . . Therefore He is able also to save forever those who draw
near to God through Him, since He always lives to make in
tercession for them."*—Heb. 7:20, 22, 25.

A BONDSMAN or guarantor
is one who stands legally liable for another, promising that a
certain duty will be faithfully performed. Jesus is the Guarantor of the New Covenant. He provides assurance for us that
God's part in the Covenant will faithfully be performed. And
He provides assurance for God that *our* part will be faithfully
performed too. If we are to live in covenant with God, everything depends upon our knowing what Jesus makes secure for
us. The more we know and trust Him, the more assured will
our faith be that its every promise and every demand will be
fulfilled. We can know that a life of faithful keeping of God's
better Covenant is indeed possible, because Jesus is the Guar-

antor of that Covenant. He makes God's faithfulness and ours *equally sure.*

We read that it was because His priesthood was confirmed by the oath of God that He became the surety or guarantee of this better Covenant. The oath of God gives us full assurance that His suretyship will secure all the better promises. The meaning and infinite value of God's oath is explained in the epistle's previous chapter: "Men swear by one greater than themselves, and with them an oath given as confirmation is an end of every dispute. In the same way God, desiring even more to show to the heirs of the promise the unchangeableness of His purpose, interposed with an oath, so that by two unchangeable things in which it is impossible for God to lie, we who have taken refuge would have strong encouragement" (Heb. 6:16–18). We thus have not only a Covenant with certain definite promises about the work of Christ but we have the living God coming in with an *oath.* Do we not begin to see that the one thing God aims at in this Covenant and asks with regard to it is our absolute confidence that He is going to do all He has promised, however difficult or amazing it may appear? *His oath is an end to all fear or doubt.* Let us come to God with an Abraham-like faith that gives Him the glory—a faith that is fully assured that what He has promised He is able to perform. The Covenant is a sealed mystery except to the person who intends without reserve to trust God and abandon himself to His word and work.

Of the work of Christ as the Guarantor of the better Covenant, our passage tells us that by means of this priesthood confirmed by oath He is able to save completely and forever (the word *panteles*—"to the uttermost" (KJV)—includes both ideas) those who come to God through Him. And this is because "He always lives to make intercession for them." As Guarantor of the Covenant, He is ceaselessly engaged in observing the believer's needs and presenting them to the Father, then receiving His answer and imparting its blessing. It is because of this never-ceasing mediation—receiving and transmitting from God to us the gifts and powers of the heavenly world—that He is able to save completely—to work and maintain in us a salvation as complete as God is willing it should be, as complete as the better Covenant has assured us it shall be. These promises are expounded (Heb. 8:7–13) as being none other than those of the New Covenant of Jeremiah, with the law written on the heart by the Spirit of God as our experience of the power of that salvation.

Jesus, the Guarantor of a better Covenant, is to be our assurance that everything connected with the Covenant is unchangeably and eternally sure. Jesus is the central point of all our communion with God, of all our prayers and desires, of all our life and walk, so that with full assurance of faith and hope we may expect every word of the Covenant to be made fully true to us by God's own power. Let us look at some of these things of which we are to be fully assured.

First, there is the love of God. The very thought of a covenant is an alliance of friendship. God's Covenant is a means of assuring us of His love, of drawing us close to His heart of love, of filling our hearts with love. This love of God is an infinite, divine energy, doing its utmost to fill the soul with itself and its blessedness. Of this love God's Son is the Messenger; of the Covenant in which God reveals it to us He is the Guarantor. Let us learn that our chief need in studying the Covenant and keeping it—in seeking and claiming its blessings—is the exercise of a strong and confident assurance in God's love.

Then there is the assurance of the sufficiency of Christ's

finished redemption. All that was needed to put away sin, to free us entirely and forever from its power, has been accomplished by Christ. His blood and death, His resurrection and ascension, have taken us out of the power of the world and transplanted us into a new life in the power of the heavenly world. All this is divine reality; Christ is surety that divine righteousness and acceptance, all-sufficient grace and strength, are ever ours. He is the guarantee that all these can and will be communicated to us in unbroken continuance.

This assurance is what we need to enter into life within the New Covenant. We shrink back, either from the surrender of all (doubting that we have the power to let it go) or from the faith for all, fearing we will never be strong or bold enough to take all that is offered us in this wonderful Covenant. But the "better" in this Covenant consists in the fact that it undertakes to provide the children of the Covenant with the very dispositions they need to accept and enjoy it. We have seen that the heart is the central object of the Covenant promise. A heart circumcised to love God fully, a heart into which God's law and fear have been put, so that it will not depart from Him—it is this that Jesus is surety of under the oath of God. Let us say it once more: the one thing God asks of us and has given the Covenant and its oath to secure is our *confident trust* that all that is needed will be done in us. This is what we dare not withhold.

I think some of us are beginning to see what has been our greatest mistake. We have thought and spoken glowingly of what Christ did on the cross, and does on the throne, as Covenant surety. And we have stopped there. But we have not expected Him to do great things *in our hearts*. And yet it is there, in the *heart*, that the consummation of the work on the cross and the throne takes place; in the *heart* the New Covenant has its full triumph. Our Guarantor is to be known not by what the mind can think of Him accomplishing in heaven but by what He does to make Himself known in the human heart. *There* is the place where His love triumphs and is enthroned. It is with the *heart* that we must believe and receive Him as the Covenant surety. Let us, with every desire we entertain in connection with the Covenant, with every duty it calls us to, with every promise it holds out, look to Jesus—under God's oath the *Guarantor* of the Covenant. Let us believe that by the Holy Spirit the heart is His home and His throne. Let us in a definite act of faith throw ourselves utterly on Him for the whole of the New Covenant life and walk. *No bondsman was ever so faithful to his undertaking as Jesus will be to His—on our behalf, in our hearts.*

And yet, despite the strong confidence and consolation the oath of God and its guarantee of the Covenant gives, there are some still looking wistfully at this blessed life, afraid to trust themselves to His wondrous grace. They have a conception of faith as something great and mighty, and they know and feel that theirs is not such. And so their feebleness remains an insuperable barrier to their inheriting the promise. Let me say once again: the act of faith by which you accept and enter this life in the New Covenant is not ordinarily an act of power but one of weakness and fear and much trembling. It is not an act in your strength but belief in a hidden strength that Jesus, the Guarantor of the Covenant, gives you. God has made Him Guarantor with the very object of inspiring us with courage and confidence. He longs, He delights to bring you into the Covenant. Why will you not bow before Him and trust Him confidently? Bow low; then look up out of your low estate to your glorified Lord, and maintain your confidence that a person who in his nothingness trusts in Him will receive more than he or she can ask or think.

Dear believer, come and *be* a believer. Believe that God is showing you how the Lord Jesus wants to have you and your life entirely for Himself; how He is willing to take charge of you entirely and work all in you; how you may even now commit yourself with all you are, and are to be, entirely to Him. If you believe, you shall see the glory of God. *What Christ has undertaken, you may confidently count upon Him to perform.*

Jesus Christ says: "*He who believes in Me,* from his innermost being will flow rivers of living water."

Chapter

12

The Book of the Covenant

"Then [Moses] took the Book of the Covenant and read it in the hearing of the people; and they said, 'All that the Lord has spoken we will do, and we will be obedient!' So Moses took the blood and sprinkled it on the people, and said, 'Behold the blood of the covenant, which the Lord has made with you in accordance with all these words.'"—Ex. 24:7 8; compare Heb. 9:18–20.

HERE IS a new aspect in which to regard God's blessed Book. Before Moses sprinkled the blood, he read the Book of the Covenant and obtained the people's acceptance of it. And when he had sprinkled it, he said, "Behold the blood of the covenant, which the Lord has made with you *in accordance with all these words.*" The Book contained all the conditions of the Covenant; only through the Book could they know all that God asked of them and all that they might ask of Him. Let us consider what new light may be thrown both upon the Covenant and upon the Book by the thought that the Bible is the Book of the Covenant.

The very first thought suggested is that in nothing will the spirit of our life and experience, as it lives either in the Old or the New Covenant, be more manifest than in our dealings with the Book. The Old had a book as well as the New. Our Bible contains both. The New was enfolded in the Old; the Old is unfolded in the New. It is possible to read the Old in the spirit of the New; it is possible to read the New as well as the Old in the spirit of the Old.

We can see this spirit of the Old most clearly in Israel when the Covenant was made. They were at once ready to promise: "All that the Lord has spoken we will do, and we will be obedient!" There was so little sense of their own sinfulness, or of the holiness and glory of God, that with perfect self-confidence they considered themselves able to undertake the keeping of the Covenant. They understood little of the meaning of that blood with which they were sprinkled or of that death and redemption of which it was the symbol. In their own strength, in the power of the flesh, they were ready to engage in the service of God. It is the same spirit in which many Christians regard the Bible—as a system of laws, a course of instruction to direct us in the way God would have us go. All He asks of us, they believe, is that we should do our utmost in seeking to fulfill its precepts. This they are sincerely ready to do. They know little or nothing about the significance of the death through which the Covenant is established, or about the resultant life from the dead through which alone a man can walk in covenant with the God of heaven.

This self-confident spirit in Israel is explained by what had happened just previously. When God had come down on Mount Sinai in thunderings and lightnings to give the law, they were greatly afraid. They said to Moses: "Speak to us yourself and we will listen; but let not God speak to us, or we will die" (Ex.

20:19). They thought it was simply a matter of hearing and knowing—they could surely obey. They did not realize that it is only the presence, and the fear, and the nearness, and the power of God humbling us that can conquer the power of sin and give the power to obey. It is so much easier to receive the instruction from man and live than to wait and hear the voice of God and die to all our own strength and goodness.

Many Christians similarly attempt to serve God without ever seeking to live in daily contact with Him, and without the faith that it is only His presence that can keep us from sin. Their religion is a matter of outward instruction from man; the waiting to hear God's voice so that they may obey Him, along with the death to the flesh and the world that comes with a close walk with God—these are unknown. They may be faithful and diligent in their study of the Bible, in reading or hearing Bible teaching; but to have as much as possible of that communion with the Covenant God Himself which makes the Christian life possible—this they do not seek.

If you would be delivered from all this, learn always to read the Book of the New Covenant in the *spirit* of the New Covenant. One of the first articles of the New Covenant has reference to this matter. When God says, "I will put My law within them and on their heart I will write it," He intends that the words of His Holy Book shall no longer be mere outward teaching but that what they command shall be our very disposition and delight, wrought in us as a birth and a life by the Holy Spirit. Every word of the New Covenant then becomes a divine assurance of what may be obtained by the Holy Spirit's working. The person learns to see that the written law brings death, that the flesh profits nothing. The study and knowledge of Bible words and thoughts cannot profit unless the Holy Spirit is waited on to make them life. The acceptance of Holy Scripture as a book of rules and the reception of these by mere human understanding will prove to be as fruitless as was Israel's response at Sinai. But as the Word of God is spoken by the living God into the heart that waits on Him, it is found to be living and powerful. It then is a word that works effectually in those who believe, giving within the heart the actual possession of the very grace about which the Word has spoken.

The New Covenant is a ministry of the Spirit (see Chapter 7). All its teaching is meant to be teaching by the Holy Spirit. The two most remarkable chapters in the Bible on the preaching of the gospel are those in which Paul expounds the secret of this teaching (1 Cor. 2; 2 Cor. 3). Every minister ought to see whether he can pass his examination in them. They tell us that in the New Covenant the Holy Spirit is everything. It is the Holy Spirit entering the heart, writing, revealing, impressing upon it God's law and truth, that alone works true obedience. No excellency of speech or human wisdom can profit in the least; God must reveal by His Holy Spirit to preacher and hearer the things He has prepared for us. What is true of the preacher is equally true of the hearer. One of the primary reasons that so many Christians never come out of the Old Covenant—never even realize that they are *in* it—is that there is so much head knowledge and no waiting for the power of the Spirit in the heart. It is only when preachers and hearers and readers believe that the Book of the New Covenant needs the *Author* of the New Covenant to explain and apply it that the Word of God can do its work.

Learn the double lesson. What God has joined together, let no man put asunder. The Bible is the Book of the New Covenant. And the Holy Spirit is the only expounder of what belongs to the Covenant. Do not expect to understand or benefit from your Bible knowledge without continually seeking the guidance of the Holy Spirit. Beware lest your earnest Bible study, your excellent books, or your beloved teachers *take the place of the Holy Spirit!* Pray daily, and perseveringly, and believingly for His teaching. He will write the Word on your heart.

The Bible is the Book of the New Covenant. Ask the Holy Spirit especially to reveal to you the New Covenant in it. It is inconceivable what loss the Church of our day is suffering because so few believers truly live as its heirs, in the true knowledge and enjoyment of its promises. In humble faith ask God to give you in all your Bible reading the spirit of wisdom and revelation, enlightening the eyes of your heart to know what are the promises that the Covenant reveals. There is divine security in Jesus, the keystone of the Covenant, and every promise will be fulfilled in you in divine power. The ministry of the Spirit, humbly waited for and listened to, will make the Book of the Covenant shine with new light—even the light of God's countenance and a full salvation.

It is quite possible that you have never yet contemplated the New Covenant as a whole, in a way that compels acceptance. Listen once again to what it really is. *True obedience and fellowship with God*—for which man was created, which sin broke off, which the law demanded but could not work, which God's own Son came from heaven to restore in our lives—*is now brought within our reach and offered us.* Our Father tells us in the Book of the New Covenant that He now expects us to live in full and unbroken obedience and communion with Him. He tells us that by the mighty power of His Son and Spirit *He Himself will work this in us*; everything has been arranged for it. He tells us that such a life of unbroken obedience *is* possible because Christ, as the Mediator, will live in us and enable us each moment to live in Him. He tells us that all He wants is simply our surrender in faith, the yielding of ourselves to Him to do His work. Oh, let us look and see this holy life, with all its powers and blessings, coming down from God in heaven, in the Son and His Spirit! Let us believe that the Holy Spirit can enable us to see and accept it as a prepared gift, to be bestowed in living power and taking possession of us. Let us look upward and look inward, with faith in the Son and the Spirit, and God will *show* us not only that every word written in the Book of the Covenant is true but also that it can be made spirit and truth within us in our daily life. *This can indeed be!*

Chapter

13

New Covenant Obedience

"Now then, if you will indeed obey My voice and keep My covenant, then you shall be My own possession among all the peoples . . . and you shall be to Me a kingdom of priests and a holy nation." —Ex. 19:5–6.

"Moreover the Lord your God will circumcise your heart and the heart of your descendants, to love the Lord your God with all your heart and with all your soul. . . . And you shall again obey the Lord, and observe all His commandments." — Deut. 30:6, 8.

"I will put My Spirit within you and cause you to walk in My statutes, and you will be careful to observe My ordinances." —Ezek. 36:27.

IN MAKING the New Covenant, God said very definitely, "Not like the covenant which I made with your fathers" (Jer. 31:32). We have learned what the problem was with that Covenant: it made God's favor dependent upon the obedience of the people. *"If you obey,* I will be your God." We have learned how the New Covenant remedied the defect: God Himself provided for the obedience. It changes

"*If you keep* My ordinances" into "I will put My Spirit within you, and *you will keep.*" Instead of the Covenant and its fulfillment depending on man's obedience, God undertakes to ensure the obedience. The Old Covenant proved the need and pointed out the path of holiness; the New inspires the love and gives the power for holiness.

In connection with this change, a serious and most dangerous mistake is often made. Because in the New Covenant obedience no longer occupies the place it had in the Old as the condition of the Covenant, and free grace has taken its place—justifying the ungodly and bestowing gifts on the rebellious—many are under the impression that obedience is *no longer as indispensable as it was then.* The error is a terrible one. The whole Old Covenant was meant to teach the lesson of the absolute and indispensable necessity of obedience for a life in God's favor. The New Covenant comes not to provide a *substitute* for that obedience but through faith to *secure* the obedience, by giving a heart that delights in it and has the power for it. And men abuse the free grace when they rest content with the grace without the obedience it is meant for. They boast of the higher privileges of the New Covenant while its chief blessing, *the power of a holy life, a heart delighting in God's law and enabled by His indwelling Spirit,* is neglected. If there is one thing we need to understand, it is the place obedience takes in the New Covenant.

Let our first thought be: *Obedience is essential.* At the very root of the relationship between a man and God, and of God's admitting him to His fellowship, lies the thought of obedience. It is the one thing God spoke of in Paradise when "the Lord God commanded the man" not to eat of the forbidden fruit. In Christ's great salvation it is the power that redeemed us:

"Through the *obedience* of the One the many will be made righteous" (Rom. 5:19). Among the promises of the New Covenant it takes first place: God means to circumcise the hearts of His people—in the removal of the body of the flesh by the circumcision of Christ—to love God with all their heart and to obey His commandments. The crowning gift of Christ's exaltation was the Holy Spirit, sent to bring salvation to us as an inward reality. The first Covenant *demanded* obedience and failed because it could not find it. The New Covenant was expressly made *to provide for obedience*. To live in the full experience of the New Covenant blessing, obedience is essential.

It is this indispensable necessity of obedience that explains why so often the entrance into the full enjoyment of the New Covenant has depended upon some single act of surrender. There was something in the life, some evil or doubtful habit, in regard to which the conscience had often said that it was not in agreement with God's perfect will. Attempts were made to push aside the troublesome suggestion. Or unbelief said it would be impossible to overcome the habit and maintain a promise of obedience to the voice within. Meantime, all our prayers appeared to be of no avail. It was as if faith could not lay hold of the blessing which was in full sight—until at last the soul agreed to regard this little thing as the test of its surrender to obey in everything and proof of its faith that in *everything* the Guarantor of the Covenant would give power to maintain the obedience. With the evil or doubtful thing given up, with a good conscience restored and the heart's confidence before God assured, the soul could receive and possess what it sought. Obedience is essential.

Obedience is possible. The thought of a demand which man cannot possibly render cuts at the very root of true hope and strength. The secret thought, "No man can obey God," throws thousands back into the Old Covenant life and into a false peace —that God does not expect more than that we do our best. Obedience *is* possible: the whole New Covenant promises and secures this.

Only understand aright what obedience means. The renewed man still has the flesh, with its fallen nature, out of which there arise involuntary evil thoughts and dispositions. These may be found in a truly obedient man. Obedience deals with the doing of what is known to be God's will, as taught by the Word and the Holy Spirit and conscience. When George Müller spoke of the great happiness he had had for more than sixty years in God's service, he attributed it two things: He had loved God's Word and "he had maintained a good conscience, not willfully going on in a course he knew to be contrary to the mind of God." When the full light of God broke in upon Gerhard Tersteegen, he wrote: "I promise, with Thy help and power, rather to give up the last drop of my blood than knowingly and willingly in my heart or my life be untrue and disobedient to Thee." Such obedience *is* an attainable degree of grace.

Yes, obedience is possible. When the law is written on the heart; when the heart is circumcised to love the Lord and to obey Him; when the love of God is shed abroad in the heart— it means that the love of God's law and of Himself has now become the moving power of our life. This love is not a vague sentiment in man's imagination of something that exists in heaven, but is a living, mighty power of God in the heart, working effectually according to His working. A life of obedience *is* possible.

This obedience is by faith. "By faith, Abraham obeyed" (Heb. 11:8). By *faith* the promises of the Covenant, the presence of the Guarantor of the Covenant, the hidden inworking of the Holy Spirit, and the love of God in His infinite desire and power to make true in us all His love and promises must *live* in us. Faith can bring them nigh and make *us* live in the very midst of *them*. Christ and His wonderful redemption need not remain at a distance from us in heaven but can become our continual experience! However cold or feeble we may feel, faith *knows* that the new heart is in us, that the love of God's law is our very nature, that the teaching and power of the Spirit are within us. Such faith knows it *can* obey. Let us hear the voice of our Savior, the Guarantor of the Covenant, as He says, with a deeper, fuller meaning than when He was on earth: "Only believe. All things are possible to him who believes."

And last of all, let us understand: *Obedience is blessedness.* Do not regard it only as *the way* to the joy and blessings of the New Covenant, but as itself, in its very *nature*, joy and happiness. To have the voice of God teaching and guiding you, to be united to God in willing what He wills, in working out what He works in you by His Spirit, in doing His holy will and pleasing Him—surely all this is joy unspeakable and full of glory!

To a healthy man it is a delight to walk or work, to put forth his strength and conquer difficulties. To a slave or a hireling it is bondage and weariness. The Old Covenant demanded obedience with an inexorable *must* and brandished the threat that followed it. The New Covenant changes the must to *can* and *may*. With confidence ask God to show you, by His Holy Spirit, how "you have been created in Christ Jesus for good works," and how, as fitted as a vine is for bearing grapes, your new nature is perfectly prepared for every good work. Ask Him to show you that He means obedience not only to be a possible thing but the most delightful and attractive gift He has to bestow—the entrance into His love and all its blessedness.

In the New Covenant the chief blessing is not the wonderful treasure of strength and grace it contains, nor the divine assurance that this treasure never can fail, but that the living God gives Himself, and makes Himself known, and takes possession of us as our God! For *this* man was created, for *this* He was redeemed, for *this* the Holy Spirit has been given and is dwelling in us. Between what God has already worked in us and what He waits to work, obedience is the blessed link. Let us seek to walk before Him in the confidence that we are of those who live in this noble and holy consciousness: My one work is to obey God.

What can be the reason, then, that so many believers have seen so little of the beauty of this New Covenant life with its power of holy and joyful obedience? Think of the disciples heading to Emmaus: "Their eyes were prevented from recognizing Jesus." The Lord was with the disciples but their hearts were blind. It is so still. It is much like Elisha's servant: all heaven is around him and he sees nothing. Nothing will help but the prayer, "O Lord, open his eyes that he may see." Lord, is there not someone who may be reading this, who just needs one touch to see it all? Oh, give that touch!

Listen, my brother. Your Father loves you with an infinite love and longs to make you, even today, His holy, happy, obedient child. He has for you an entirely different life from what you are living. It is a life in which His grace shall actually work in you every moment all He asks you to be. A life of childlike obedience, doing daily what the Father shows you to be His will. A life in which the abiding love of your Father, and the abiding presence of your Savior, and the joy of the Holy Spirit, can keep you and make you glad and strong.

This is *His* message. This life is for *you*. Fear not to accept this life, to give yourself to it and its entire obedience. *In Christ it is possible, it is sure!*

Turn heavenward and ask the Father to show you this blessed spiritual life. Ask and expect it. Keep your eyes *fixed* upon it. *The great blessing of the New Covenant is obedience; the wonderful power to will and do as God wills.* It is indeed the entrance to every other blessing. It is Paradise restored and heaven opened—the creature honoring his Creator, the Creator delighting in His creature; the child glorifying the Father, the Father glorifying the child, as He changes him from one degree of glory to another, into the likeness of His Son.

Chapter

14

⸻

The New Covenant:
A Covenant of Grace

"Sin shall not be master over you, for you are not under law but under grace."—Rom. 6:14.

THE WORDS "Covenant of grace," though not found in Scripture, are the correct expression of the truth it abundantly teaches: that the contrast between the two Covenants is none other than that of law and grace. Of the New Covenant, grace is the great characteristic: "The law came in so that the transgression would increase; but where sin increased, grace abounded all the more" (Rom. 5:20). It was to bring the Romans entirely away from living under the Old Covenant and to teach them their place in the New that Paul wrote: "You are not under law but under grace." And he assures them that if they believe this, and live in it, their experience would confirm God's promise: "Sin shall not be master over you." What the law could not do—give deliverance from the power of sin over us—grace would effect. The New Covenant was entirely a Covenant of grace. In the wonderful grace of God it had its origin; it was meant to be a manifestation of the riches and the glory of that grace. As the result of grace, and by grace working in us, all its promises can be fulfilled and experienced.

The word *grace* is used in two senses. It is first the gracious disposition in God *that moves Him* to love us freely without our merit and to bestow all His blessings upon us. Then it also means that power through which this grace does its work *in us*. The redeeming work of Christ and the righteousness He won for us, equally with the work of the Spirit in us and the power of the new life He brings, are spoken of as "grace." It includes all that Christ has done and still does, all He has and gives, all He is *for* us and *in* us. John says, "We saw His glory, glory as of the only begotten from the Father, full of grace and truth." "The law was given through Moses; grace and truth were realized through Jesus Christ." "For of His fullness we have all received, and grace upon grace." What the law demands, grace supplies.

The contrast that John pointed out is expounded by Paul: "The law came in so that the transgression would increase" and the way be prepared for the abounding of grace more exceedingly. The law points the way but gives no strength to walk in it. The law demands, but makes no provision for its demands being met. The law burdens and condemns and slays. It can awaken desire but cannot satisfy it. It can rouse to effort but cannot secure success. It can appeal to motives, but it gives no inward power beyond what man himself has. And so, while warring against sin, it became its very ally in giving the sinner over to a hopeless condemnation. "The power of sin is the law" (1 Cor. 15:56).

To deliver us from the bondage and the dominion of sin,

grace reached its peak through Jesus Christ. Its work is twofold. Its exceeding abundance is seen in the free and full pardon there is of all transgression, in the bestowal of a perfect righteousness, and in the believer's acceptance into God's favor and friendship. "In Him we have redemption through His blood, the forgiveness of our trespasses, according to the riches of His grace" (Eph. 1:7). It is not only at conversion and our admittance into God's favor but throughout all our life, at each step of our way and amidst the highest attainments of the most advanced saint. We owe everything to grace and grace alone. The thought of merit and work and worthiness is completely excluded.

The exceeding abundance of grace is equally seen in the work that the Holy Spirit every moment maintains within us. We have found that the central blessing of the New Covenant, flowing from Christ's redemption and the pardon of our sins, is the new heart in which God's law and reverence and love have been put. It is in the fulfillment of this promise, *in the maintenance of the heart in a state of fitness for God's indwelling*, that the glory of grace is especially seen. In the very nature of things this must be so. Paul writes: "Where sin increased, grace abounded all the more." And where, as far as I was concerned, did sin increase? All the sin in earth and hell could not harm me were it not for its presence in my heart. It is there it has exercised its terrible dominion. And it is there the exceeding abundance of grace must be proved if it is to benefit me. All the grace in earth and heaven could not help me; it is only in the *heart* it can be received and known and enjoyed. "Where sin increased"—in the heart—there "grace abounded all the more, so that, as sin reigned in death," working its destruction in the heart and life, "even so grace would reign," in the heart too, "through righteousness to eternal life through Jesus Christ our Lord" (Rom.

5:21). As had been said just before, "Those who receive the abundance of grace and of the gift of righteousness will reign in life through the One, Jesus Christ" (Rom. 5:17).

Of this reign of grace in the heart Scripture speaks wondrous things. Paul speaks of the grace that fitted him for his work, of "the gift of God's grace which was given to me according to the working of His power" (Eph. 3:7). "The grace of our Lord was more than abundant, with the faith and love which are found in Christ Jesus" (1 Tim. 1:14). "His *grace* toward me did not prove vain; but *I labored even more* than all of them, yet not I, but *the grace* of God with me" (1 Cor. 15:10). "He has said to me, '*My grace* is sufficient for you, for power is perfected in weakness'" (2 Cor. 12:9).

He speaks in the same way of grace as working in the life of the believers when he exhorts them to "be strong in the grace that is in Christ Jesus" (2 Tim. 2:1); when he tells us of "the grace of God" in the Corinthians; when he encourages them: "God is able to make all grace abound to you, so that . . . you may have an abundance for every good deed" (2 Cor. 9:8). Grace is not only the power that moves the heart of God in its compassion toward us when He acquits the sinner and makes him a child, but is equally the power that moves the heart of the saint and provides it each moment with the disposition and the power which it needs to love God and to do His will.

It is impossible to speak too strongly of the need to know that as wonderful and free and sufficient as is the grace that pardons, so is the grace that sanctifies. We are just as absolutely dependent upon the latter as the former. The grace that works in us must as exclusively do all in us and through us as the grace that pardons does all for us. In the one case as in the other, everything is by faith alone. Not to understand this brings a double danger. On the one hand, people think that grace cannot be more exalted than in the bestowal of pardon on the vile and unworthy, and a secret feeling arises that if God is so magnified by our sins we must not expect to be freed from them in this life. With many this cuts at the root of the life of true holiness. On the other hand, from not knowing that grace is always and alone to do all the work in our sanctification and fruit-bearing, men are thrown upon their own efforts. Their life remains one of feebleness and bondage under the law, and they never yield themselves to allowing grace to do all it would.

Let us listen to what God's Word says: "*By grace* you have been saved *through faith* . . . not as a result of works, so that no one may boast. For we are His workmanship, created *in Christ Jesus* for good works, which God prepared beforehand so that we would walk in them" (Eph. 2:8–10). Grace stands in contrast to good works of our own not only before conversion but after conversion. We are created *in Christ Jesus* for good works, which God has prepared beforehand for us. It is grace alone that can work them in us and work them out through us. Not only the commencement but also the continuance of the Christian life is the work of grace. "But if it is by grace, it is no longer on the basis of works, otherwise grace is no longer grace" (Rom. 11:6). As we see that grace is literally and absolutely to do all in us, so that all our actions are the showing forth of grace in us, we shall agree to live the life of faith—a life in which, every moment, everything is expected from God. It is only then that we shall experience that sin shall not, never, not for a moment, be master over us.

"You are not under law but under grace." There are three possible lives: one entirely under law; one entirely under grace; one a mixed life, partly law and partly grace. It is this last against which Paul warns the Romans. It is this which is so common and works such ruin among Christians. Let us ask ourselves if this is not our position and the cause of our low state. Let us ask God to open our eyes to see that in the New Covenant everything—every movement, every moment of our Christian life—is to be of grace—grace abounding exceedingly and working mightily. Let us believe that our Covenant God waits to cause all grace to abound toward us. And let us begin to live the life of faith that depends upon, trusts in, looks to, and ever waits for God, through Jesus Christ, by the Holy Spirit, to work in us that which is pleasing in His sight.

May grace and peace be yours in fullest measure.

Chapter

15

―――

The Covenant of
a Perpetual Priesthood

*"My covenant with [Levi] was one of life and peace, and
I gave them to him as an object of reverence; so he revered Me
and stood in awe of My name. True instruction was in his
mouth, and unrighteousness was not found on his lips; he
walked with Me in peace and uprightness, and he turned many
back from iniquity."*—Mal. 2:5–6.

ISRAEL WAS meant by God
to be a nation of priests. In the first making of the Covenant
this was distinctly stipulated: "If you will indeed obey My voice
and keep My covenant, then . . . you shall be to Me a kingdom
of priests" (Ex. 19:5–6). They were to be the stewards of the
utterances of God, the channels through whom God's knowledge and blessing were to be communicated to the world. In
them all nations were to be blessed.

Within the people of Israel one tribe was specially set apart
to embody and emphasize the priestly idea. Normally, all first-
born sons would have been priests, but to secure a more com-

plete separation of priests from the rest of the people and to stress the giving up of other pursuits, God chose one tribe to be devoted exclusively to the work of proving what constitutes the spirit and the power of priesthood. Just as the priesthood of all the people was part of God's Covenant with them, so the special calling of Levi is spoken of as God's Covenant of life and peace. This was meant to be a picture to help them and us, in some measure, to understand the priesthood of His own blessed Son, the Mediator of the New Covenant.

Like Israel, all God's people under the New Covenant are a royal priesthood. The right of free and full access to God, the duty and power of mediating for our fellow men and being God's channel of blessing to them, is the inalienable birthright of every believer. However, owing to the weakness and incapacity of many of God's children and their ignorance of the mighty grace of the New Covenant, they are utterly impotent to take up and exercise their priestly functions. To remedy this lack of service and to show forth the exceeding riches of His grace in the New Covenant, God still allows and invites those of His redeemed ones who are willing to offer their lives to this blessed ministry. For those who accept the call, the New Covenant brings in special measure what God has said: "My covenant with him is one of life and peace." It becomes to them in very deed "the Covenant of a perpetual priesthood" (Num. 25:13). As the Covenant of Levi's priesthood issued and culminated in Christ's, ours issues from that again and receives from it its blessing to dispense to the world.

To those who desire to know the conditions on which, as part of the New Covenant, the Covenant of a perpetual priesthood can be received and carried out, a study of the conditions on which Levi received the priesthood will be most instructive.

We are told not only that God chose that tribe, but also why He did so. Malachi says: "He revered Me and stood in awe of My name." The reference is to what took place at Sinai when Israel had made the golden calf. Moses called all who were on the Lord's side, who were ready to avenge the dishonor done to God, to come to him. The tribe of Levi did so and at his bidding took their swords and slew three thousand of the idolatrous people (Ex. 32:26–29). In the blessing with which Moses blessed the tribes before his death, Levi's absolute devotion to God without considering relative or friend is mentioned as the proof of their fitness for God's service: "Let Your Thummim and Your Urim belong to Your godly man . . . who said of his father and his mother, 'I did not consider them'; and he did not acknowledge his brothers, nor did he regard his own sons; for they observed Your word and kept Your covenant" (Deut. 33:8–9).

The same principle is strikingly illustrated in the story of Aaron's grandson Phinehas, where he, in his zeal for God, executed judgment on disobedience to God's command. The words are most suggestive. "Then the Lord spoke to Moses, saying, 'Phinehas the son of Eleazar, the son of Aaron the priest, has turned away My wrath from the sons of Israel in that *he was jealous with My jealousy* among them, so that I did not destroy the sons of Israel in My jealousy. Therefore say, "Behold, I give him My covenant of peace; and it shall be for him and his descendants after him, a covenant of a perpetual priesthood, because *he was jealous for his God* and made atonement for the sons of Israel"'" (Num. 25:10–13). To be jealous with God's jealousy, to be jealous for God's honor and rise up against sin, is the gate into the Covenant of a perpetual priesthood. It is the secret of being entrusted by God with the sacred work of teaching His people, of burning incense before Him, and of turning many from unrighteousness (Deut. 33:10; Mal. 2:6).

Even the New Covenant is in danger of being abused by the seeking of our own happiness or holiness more than the honor of God or the deliverance of men. Even where these are not entirely neglected, they do not always take the place they are meant to have—that first place which makes everything, even the dearest and best, secondary and subordinate to the work of helping and blessing men. A reckless disregarding of everything that would interfere with God's will and commands, a being jealous with God's jealousy against sin, a witnessing and a fighting against it at any sacrifice—these are requisites in the school of training for the priestly office.

It is this the world needs today: men of God in whom the fire of God burns, men who can stand and speak and act powerfully on behalf of a God who among His own people is dishonored by the worship of the golden calf. Look at the place given to money and to the wealthy in the church, at the prevalence of worldliness and luxury, or the more subtle danger of a worship meant for the true God but under forms taken from the Egyptians and suited to the wisdom and the carnal life of this world. An outward form of religion that God cannot approve is often found even where the people still profess to be in covenant with God. "Dedicate yourselves today to the Lord— for every man has been against his son and against his brother— in order that He may bestow a blessing upon you today" (Ex. 32:29). This call of Moses is as much needed today as ever. To each one who responds there is the reward of the priesthood.

Let all who would know completely what the New Covenant means remember God's Covenant of life and peace with Levi. Accepting the holy calling to be an intercessor involves continual petition and sacrifice before the Lord. Love, work, pray, and believe as one whom God has sought and found to stand in the gap before Him. The New Covenant was dedicated by a sacrifice and a death: consider it your most wonderful privilege, your fullest entrance into a meaningful life. You are called to reflect the glory of the Lord and to be transformed into the same image from glory to glory by the Spirit of the Lord, letting the spirit of Christ's sacrifice and death be the moving power in all your priestly functions. *Sacrifice yourself— live and die for your fellow men.*

One of the primary purposes for which God has made a Covenant with us is, as we have said so often, to awaken strong confidence in Himself and His faithfulness to His promise. And one of the objects that He has in awakening and so strengthening the faith in us is that He may use us as His channels of blessing to the world. In the work of saving men, He wants intercessory prayer to take the first place. He would have us come to Him to receive from Him the spiritual life and power that can flow out from us to the world. He knows how difficult and hopeless it is in many cases to deal with sinners. He knows that it is no small thing for us to believe that in answer to our prayer the mighty power of God will move to save those around us. He knows that it takes strong faith to persevere patiently in prayer in cases in which the answer is long delayed. And so He undertakes, in experiences He sends our way, to manifest and prove what faith in His divine power can do in bringing down all the blessings of the New Covenant on ourselves, that we may be able to expect confidently what we petition for others.

In our priestly life there is still another aspect. The priests were given no inheritance like that given their brothers; the Lord God was their inheritance. They had access to His dwelling and His presence so that there they might intercede and then testify to what God is and what He wills. Their personal privileges and experiences fitted them for their work. If we would intercede with power, we must live in the full realization of New Covenant life. It gives us not only liberty and confidence with God and power to persevere, it gives us power with men— for we can prove and testify to what God has done for us. Herein is the full glory of the New Covenant, that, like Christ, its Mediator, we have the fire of the divine love dwelling in us and consuming us in the service of men. May we each realize that the chief glory of the New Covenant is that it is the Covenant of a perpetual priesthood.

Chapter

16

The Ministry of the New Covenant

"You are our letter, written in our hearts, known and read by all men; being manifested that you are a letter of Christ, cared for by us, written not with ink but with the Spirit of the living God, not on tablets of stone but on tablets of human hearts. Such confidence have we through Christ toward God. Not that we are adequate in ourselves to consider anything as coming from ourselves, but our adequacy is from God, who also made us adequate as servants of a new covenant, not of the letter but of the Spirit; for the letter kills, but the Spirit gives life."—2 Cor. 3:2–6.

WE HAVE seen that the New Covenant is a ministry of the Spirit. The Holy Spirit ministers all its grace and blessing in divine power and life.* He does this through men, men who are called servants of a New Covenant, ministers of the Spirit. Both the divine execution of the Covenant with regard to men and the earthly ministry of God's servants are to be in the power of the Holy Spirit. The ministry

---

* It may be well to read again and compare Chapter 7: "The New Covenant: A Ministry of the Spirit."

of the New Covenant has its glory and its fruit in this, that it is all to be a demonstration of the Spirit and of power.

What a contrast this is to the Old Covenant. Moses indeed received a portion of the glory of God shining upon him, but then had to put a veil on his face. Israel was incapable of looking on the glory. When they and later generations either heard or read the words of Moses, there was often a veil on their hearts. From Moses they might receive knowledge and thoughts and desires, but the power of God's Spirit, to enable them to see the full glory of what God speaks, was not yet given. The exceeding glory of the New Covenant is that it is a ministry of the Spirit; that its servants have their sufficiency from God who makes them ministers of the Spirit—makes them able so to speak the words of God in the Spirit that they are written in the human heart. The result is that the hearers become living letters from Christ, manifesting the law written in their hearts and lives.

The ministry of the Spirit! What a glory there is in it! What a responsibility it brings! What a sufficiency of grace is provided for it! What a privilege to be a minister of the Spirit!

We have tens of thousands throughout Christendom who are called ministers of the gospel. What an inconceivable influence they exert for life or for death over the millions who depend upon them for their knowledge and participation in the Christian life. What a power there would be if all these were ministers of the Spirit! Let us study the Word until we see what God meant this ministry to be, and learn to take our part in praying and laboring to have it nothing less.

God has made us servants of the Spirit. The first thought is that a minister of the New Covenant must be a man personally *possessed* by the Holy Spirit. There is a twofold work of the Spirit: one in giving a holy disposition and character, the other in qualifying and empowering the person for work. The former must always come first. The promise of Christ to His disciples that they would receive the Holy Spirit for their service was very definitely given to those who had followed and loved Him and had kept His commandments. It is by no means enough that a man has been born of the Spirit. If he is to be an "adequate servant" of the New Covenant, he must know what it is to be led by the Spirit, to walk in the Spirit, and to say, "The law of the Spirit of life in Christ Jesus has set me free from the law of sin and death" (Rom. 8:2).

What person wanting to learn Greek or Hebrew would accept a professor who hardly knows the basic elements of these languages? And how can a man be a servant of the New Covenant—which is so entirely "a ministry of the Spirit," a ministering of heavenly life and power—unless he knows by experience what it is to live by the Spirit? The minister must be, before everything else, a personal proof and witness of the truth and power of God in the fulfillment of what the New Covenant promises. Ministers are to be select men—the best examples of what the Holy Spirit can do to sanctify a man and to equip him for His service by the working of God's power in him.

God has made us servants of the Spirit. Next comes the truth that all the *work* done by these servants can be done in the power of the Spirit. What an unspeakably precious assurance: Christ sends them to do a heavenly work, to do *His* work, to be the instruments in *His* hands, by which *He* works. He clothes them with a *heavenly* power. Their calling is to "preach the gospel . . . by the Holy Spirit sent from heaven" (1 Pet. 1:12). As far as feelings are concerned, they may have to say as did Paul: "I was with you in weakness and in fear and in much trem-

bling" (1 Cor. 2:3). That does not prevent their adding, nay
rather, that just may be the secret of their being able to add:
"My message and my preaching . . . were in demonstration of
the Spirit and of power" (v. 4). If a man is to be a servant of the
New Covenant—a messenger and a teacher of its true blessings
so as to lead God's children to live in it—nothing less will do
than a full experience of its power in himself as the Spirit ministers it. Whether in his feeding on God's Word himself or his
seeking in it for God's message for his people, whether in pri-
vate or intercessory prayer, whether in counseling or public
teaching, he is to wait upon, to receive, to yield to the energiz-
ing of the Holy Spirit as the mighty power of God working
with him. This is his sufficiency for the work. He may every
day afresh claim and receive the anointing of the Holy Spirit,
the new inbreathing from Christ of His own spirit and life.

God has made us servants of the Spirit. There is something
still of no less importance. The servant of the Spirit must see to
it that *he leads others to the Holy Spirit.* Many will ask, "If the
minister is led by the Spirit in teaching his flock, is that not
enough?" By no means. Men may become too dependent on
him; men may see him as their chief source for edification or as
their ministry-model and, seeing the evident power and blessing in his ministry, have reason to wonder that their results are
not more definitely spiritual and permanent. The reason is
simple: the Father wants every child to *live in direct, continual
fellowship with Himself.* This cannot be unless each one is taught
and helped to personally know and wait on the Holy Spirit.
Bible study and prayer, faith, love and obedience—the whole
daily walk—must be taught as entirely dependent on the teaching and working of the indwelling Spirit.

The servant of the Spirit very definitely and perseveringly

points away from himself to the Spirit. This is what John the Baptist did. He was filled with the Holy Spirit from his birth, but he sent men away from himself to Christ. Christ did the same. In His farewell discourse He called His disciples to turn from His personal instruction to the inward teaching of the Holy Spirit, who would dwell in them and guide them into the truth and power of all He had taught them.

There is nothing so needed in Christ's Church today. All its feebleness, formalities and worldliness along with the lack of holiness, of personal devotion to the Savior, and of enthusiasm for His cause and kingdom, is owing to one thing—the Holy Spirit is not known and honored and yielded to as the all-sufficient source of a holy life. The New Covenant is not known as a ministry of the Spirit in the heart of every believer. The one thing needful for the Church is the Holy Spirit in His power dwelling and ruling in the lives of God's saints. And a primary need is for pastors themselves to be ministers of the Spirit, living in the enjoyment and power of this great gift, persistently laboring to bring those whom they shepherd into the possession of their birthright. The ministering *of* the Spirit makes ministry *by* the Spirit possible and effectual. And ministry *by* the Spirit again makes the ministering *of* the Spirit an actual reality in the life of the Church.

We know how dependent the Church is on its shepherds. The converse is no less true. The ministers are dependent on the Church! They too are its children: they breathe its atmosphere; they share its health or sickliness; they are dependent upon its fellowship and intercession. Let none of us think that all that the New Covenant calls us to is to see that we personally accept and rejoice in its blessings. No, indeed! God wants everyone who enters into it to know that its privileges are for all

His children, and to spread this truth. And there is no more effectual way of doing this than taking thought for the ministry of the Church. Compare the ministry around you with its pattern in God's Word (1 Cor. 2; 2 Cor. 3). Join with others who understand the goal of the New Covenant—that it is a ministry of the Spirit—and call upon God for a spiritual ministry. Ask the Holy Spirit to teach you what you can do to have the ministry of your local church become a truly spiritual one.

Human condemnation will do as little good as human commendation. It is necessary that the supreme place of the Holy Spirit, as the representative and revealer of the Father and the Son, become clear to us. Then the one desire of our heart, and our continual prayer, will be that God may reveal to all the ministers of His Word their heavenly calling so that they may, above all, seek this one thing—to be competent ministers of the New Covenant, not of the letter, but of the Spirit.

Chapter

17

His Holy Covenant

"To remember His holy covenant . . . to grant us that we, being rescued from the hand of our enemies, might serve Him without fear, in holiness and righteousness before Him all our days."—Luke 1:72–75.

WHEN ZACHARIAS was filled with the Holy Spirit and prophesied, he spoke about God's visiting and redeeming His people as a remembering of His holy Covenant. He spoke of what the blessings of that Covenant would be, not in words that had been used before but in what was manifestly a divine revelation to him by the Holy Spirit, and he gathered up all the former promises in these words: "That we might serve Him without fear, *in holiness and righteousness before Him all our days.*" Holiness in life and service is to be the great gift of the Covenant of God's holiness. As we have seen before, the Old Covenant proclaimed and demanded holiness; the New provides it. Holiness of heart and life is its great blessing.

There is no attribute of God so difficult to define, so uniquely a matter of divine revelation, so mysterious, incomprehensible, and inconceivably glorious, as His holiness. It is that by which He is specifically worshiped in His majesty on the throne of heaven (Isa. 6:3; Rev. 4:8,15:4). It unites His righteousness, that judges and condemns, with His love, that saves and blesses. As the Holy One He is a consuming fire (Isa. 10:17); as the Holy One He also loves to dwell among His people (Isa. 12:6). As the Holy One He is at an infinite distance from us; as the Holy One He comes inconceivable near, and makes us one with and like Himself. The chief purpose of His holy Covenant is to make us holy as He is holy.

As the Holy One He says: "I am holy; you shall be holy. I am the Lord who sanctifies you, who makes you holy." The highest conceivable summit of blessedness is our being partakers of the divine nature, of the divine holiness.

This is the great blessing that Christ, the Mediator of the New Covenant, brings. He has become to us "wisdom from God, and righteousness and sanctification" (1 Cor. 1:30)—righteousness in order to produce, and as a preparation for, sanctification or holiness.* He prayed to the Father: "Sanctify them in the truth. . . . For their sakes I *sanctify* Myself, that they themselves also may be sanctified in truth" (John 17:17,19). In Him we are *sanctified*, saints, holy ones (Rom. 1:7; 1 Cor. 1:2). We have "put on the new self, which in the likeness of God is created in righteousness and holiness of the truth" (Eph. 4:24). *Holiness* is our very nature.

We are holy in Christ. As we believe it, as we receive it, as we yield ourselves to the truth and have this holiness revealed to us during fellowship with Him, its fountainhead, we shall know how divinely true it is.

---

* Remember that the words "sanctify," "sanctity," and "saint" are the same as "make holy," "holiness," and "holy one."

It is for this purpose that the Holy Spirit has been given in our hearts. He is the "Spirit of holiness." His every working is in the power of holiness. Paul says: "God has *chosen you from the beginning* for salvation *through sanctification by the Spirit* and faith in the truth" (2 Thess. 2:13). As simple and entire as is our dependence on the word of truth, the external means, so must be our confidence in the hidden power for holiness which the working of the Spirit brings. The connection between God's electing purpose and the work of the Spirit through the word we obey comes out with equal clearness in Peter: "*Chosen . . . by the sanctifying work of the Spirit*, to obey Jesus Christ" (1 Pet. 1:2). The Holy Spirit is the Spirit of the life of Christ; as we know and honor and trust Him, we shall learn and experience that in the New Covenant sanctification is our covenantal right. We shall be assured that as God has promised, so He will work it in us that we "might serve Him without fear, in holiness and righteousness before Him all our days." With a treasure of holiness in Christ and the very Spirit of holiness in our hearts, *we can live holy lives*. That is, if we believe Him "who works in us both to will and to work" (Phil. 2:13).

In the light of this Covenant promise, with the blessed Son and the Holy Spirit to work it out in us, what new meaning is given to the teaching of the New Testament! Take the first epistle Paul wrote. It was directed to men who only a few months previously had been turned from idols to serve the living God and to wait for His Son from heaven. The words he speaks in regard to the holiness they might aim at and expect—because God was going to work it in them—are so *grand* that many Christians pass them by as practically unintelligible (1 Thess. 3:12–13): "May the Lord cause you to increase and abound in love . . . so that *He may establish your hearts without blame in*

holiness before our God and Father at the coming of our Lord
Jesus with all His saints." That promises holiness, unblamable
holiness, a heart without blame in holiness—a heart established
in all this by God Himself. Paul might indeed say of a word like
this: "Who has believed our report?" He had written of himself
(2:10): "You are witnesses . . . how *devoutly* and *uprightly* and
blamelessly we behaved toward you believers." He assures them
that what God has done for him He will do for them—give
them hearts unblameable in holiness. The Church believes so
little in the mighty power of God and the truth of His holy
Covenant that the grace of such heart-holiness is hardly spoken
of. The verse is often quoted in connection with "the coming of
our Lord Jesus with all His saints"; but its real point is that
when He comes, we may meet Him with *hearts established without blame in holiness* by God Himself. All too little is this understood or proclaimed or expected.

Or take another verse in 1 Thessalonians (5:23), also spoken to these young converts from heathenism in reference to
the coming of our Lord. Some think that to speak much of the
coming of the Lord will make us holy. Alas, how little it has
done so in many cases. It is the New Covenant holiness, wrought
by God Himself in us, believed in and waited for from Him,
that can make our waiting differ from the carnal expectations
of the Jews or the disciples. Listen—"NOW MAY THE GOD OF
PEACE HIMSELF"—that is the keynote of the New Covenant:
what you never can do, God will work in you— "SANCTIFY YOU
ENTIRELY." This you may ask and expect: "*and may your spirit
and soul and body be preserved complete*, WITHOUT BLAME *at the
coming of our Lord Jesus Christ.*" And now, as if to meet the
doubt that will arise: "*Faithful is He who calls you*, and He also
will bring it to pass" (v. 24). What has not entered into the

heart of man, God will work in those that wait for Him. Until the Church sees and believes that our holiness is to be the *continuous, almighty working of the Three-One God in us,* and that our spiritual life must be an unceasing receiving of it direct from Himself, these promises remain a sealed book.

Let us now return to the prophecy of the Holy Spirit by Zacharias of God's remembering the Covenant of His holiness, to make us holy, to establish our hearts unblamable in holiness, that we might serve Him in holiness and righteousness. Note how every word is significant.

To grant us. It is to be a gift from above. The promise given with the Covenant was: "I the Lord have spoken it; *I will perform it.*" We need to beseech God both to *show* us what He will do and *to do it.* When our faith expects all from Him, the blessing will be found.

That we, being rescued from the hand of our enemies. He had said just before: "*He has raised up a horn of salvation for us . . . salvation from our enemies, and from the hand of all who hate us*" (Luke 1:69 71). It is only a free people who can serve a holy God or be holy. It is only as the teaching of Romans 6–8 is experienced and we know what it is to be "freed from sin" and "freed from the law," and that "the Spirit of life in Christ Jesus has set me free from the law of sin and of death," that, in perfect liberty from every power that could hinder, I can expect God to do His mighty work in me.

Might serve Him. My servant does not serve me by spending all his time in getting himself ready *for* work but in *doing* my work. The holy Covenant sets us free and endows us with divine grace that God may have us for His work—the same work Christ began and we now carry on.

Without fear. In childlike confidence and boldness before

God. And before men too. A freedom from fear in every difficulty, because having learned that God works all in us we can
trust Him to work all for us and through us.

Before Him. With His continued presence all the day, as the
unceasing security of our obedience and our fearlessness, the
never-failing secret of our being sanctified wholly.

All our days. Not only all the day for one day, but for every
day, because Jesus is a High Priest with the power of an endless
life; and the mighty operation of God as promised in the Covenant is as unchanging as is God Himself.

Have you begun to see that God's Word promises far more
than you ever expected? It is well that it should be so. It is only
when you begin to say, "Glory to Him who is able to do far
more abundantly beyond all that we ask or think," and expect
God's almighty, supernatural, altogether immeasurable power
and grace to work out the New Covenant life in you, and *to
make you holy*, that you will really come to the place of helplessness and dependence where God can work.

Let us believe that God's Word is true and say with Zacharias,
"Blessed be the Lord God of Israel, for He has visited His people
. . . to remember HIS HOLY COVENANT, to grant us that we, being rescued from the hand of our enemies, might serve Him
without fear, *in holiness and righteousness before Him all our days.*"

18

Entering the Covenant:
With All the Heart

"And they entered into the covenant to seek the Lord God of their fathers with all their heart and soul."—2 Chron. 15:12 (see 34:31, and 2 Kings 23:3).

"The Lord your God will circumcise your heart . . . to love the Lord your God with all your heart and with all your soul."—Deut. 30:6.

"I will give them a heart to know Me, for I am the Lord; and they will be My people, and I will be their God, for they will return to Me with their whole heart."—Jer. 24:7 (see 29:13).

"I will make an everlasting covenant with them that I will not turn away from them, to do them good; and I will put the fear of Me in their hearts so that they will not turn away from Me. I will rejoice over them to do them good . . . with all My heart and with all My soul."—Jer. 32:40–41.

IN THE DAYS of Asa, Hezekiah, and Josiah, we read of Israel entering into "the covenant" with their whole heart, "to perform the words of the covenant written in this book" (2 Chron. 34:31). Of Asa's day, we read: "They made an oath to the Lord. . . . All Judah rejoiced concerning the oath, for they had sworn *with their whole heart* and had sought Him *earnestly*, and He let them find Him" (2 Chron. 15:14–15). Wholeheartedness is the secret of entering the Covenant and of God's being found in it. Wholeheartedness is the secret of joy in salvation—a full entrance into all the blessedness the Covenant brings. God rejoices over His people to do them good *with His whole heart and His whole soul*; conversely it requires *our whole heart and our whole soul* to enter into and enjoy this joy of God in doing us good with His whole heart and His whole soul. With whatever measure we take part, it will be measured out to us.

If we have at all understood the teaching of God's Word in regard to the New Covenant, we know what it reveals in regard to the two parties who meet in it. On God's side there is the promise to do for us and in us all that we need to serve and to enjoy Him. He rejoices in doing us good with His whole heart. He will be our God, doing for us all that a God can do, giving Himself as God to be fully ours. And on our side there is the prospect held out of our being able, in the power of what He engages to do, to "turn to Him with our whole heart," "to love Him with all our heart and all our strength." The first and great commandment, the only possible terms on which God can fully reveal Himself, is, "You shall love the Lord your God with all your heart" (Deut. 6:5). That law is unchangeable. The New

Covenant brings us the grace to obey by lifting us into the love of God and enabling us, by faith, to yield ourselves wholeheartedly and courageously to the God of the Covenant and to embrace life in His service.

Wholeheartedness in love for and service to God! How shall I speak of it? Need I point out its imperative *necessity*? It is the one unalterable condition of true communion with God, and nothing else can suffice. Must I speak of its infinite *reasonableness*? With such a God—the very fountain of all that is loving and lovely, of all that is good and blessed, the all-glorious God—surely there cannot for a moment be a thought of our consenting to offer Him anything less than the love of the whole heart. Ought I to stress its unspeakable *blessedness*? To love Him with the whole heart—this is the only possible way of receiving His great love into our heart and of rejoicing in it. How wonderful to yield oneself to that mighty love and allow God Himself, just as an earthly love enters into us and makes us glad, to give us the taste and the joy of the heavenliness of that love. Or shall I stress its terrible *lack*? Yes, what shall I say about this? Where can one find words to open the eyes and reach the heart and show how widespread is the lack of true wholeheartedness in the faith, in the desire to love God with the whole heart, in the sacrifice of everything to possess Him, to please Him, to be wholly possessed by Him? And shall I not mention the blessed *certainty of its attainableness*? The Covenant has provided for it! The Triune God will work it by taking possession of the heart and dwelling there. The blessed Mediator of the Covenant undertakes for all we have to do. His constraining love shed abroad in our hearts by the Holy Spirit can bring it and maintain it. Yes, I ask, how shall I adequately speak of all this?

Have we not spoken enough of it already in this book? Do

we not need something more than words and thoughts? Is not what we need rather this—to turn quietly to the Holy Spirit who dwells in us and, with faith in the light and the strength our Lord gives through Him, to *accept* and *act out* what God tells us about the circumcised heart He has placed within us and the God-wrought wholeheartedness He works? Surely the new heart which has been given us to love God with—the heart with God's Spirit in it—is wholly for God! Let our faith accept and rejoice in this wondrous gift and not fear to say: "I *will* love You, O Lord, with my *whole* heart."

Just think for a moment about what it means that God has given us such a heart.

God's giving is for our good. But His giving depends on our *taking.* He does not force upon us spiritual possessions. He promises and gives in such measure as desire and faith are ready to *receive.* He gives in divine power; as faith yields itself to that power and accepts the gift, it becomes consciously and experientially our possession.

As spiritual gifts, *God's bestowings are not recognized by sense or reason.* "As it is written: 'Things which eye has not seen and ear has not heard, and which have not entered the heart of man, *all that* God has prepared for those who love Him.' For to us God revealed them *through the Spirit.* . . . Now we have *received* . . . the Spirit who is from God, so that we may *know* the things freely given to us by God" (1 Cor. 2:9–12). It is as you yield yourself to be led and taught by the Spirit that your faith will be able, despite all lack of feeling, to rejoice in the possession of the new heart and all that is given with it.

Then, *this divine giving is continuous.* I bestow a gift on a man; he takes it, and I may never see him again. God regularly bestows temporal gifts on men, and they never even think of

Him. But *spiritual gifts* are to be received and enjoyed only through unceasing communication with God Himself. The new heart is not a power I have in myself, like the natural endowments of thinking or loving. No, it is only through unceasing dependence upon God that the heavenly gift of a new heart can be maintained uninjured day by day and become stronger. It is only because of God's immediate, continuous presence, with unbroken dependence on Him, that spiritual endowments are preserved.

Then, further, *spiritual gifts can be enjoyed only by acting them out in faith.* None of the graces of the Christian life (love, meekness, boldness, etc.) can be felt or known, much less strengthened, until we begin to exercise them. We must not wait to feel them or sense the strength for them; we must, in obedience to the faith that they have been given to us by God, begin to *practice* them. Whatever we read about the new heart and God's devoted investment to it in the New Covenant must be boldly believed and put into action.

All this is especially true of wholeheartedness and loving God with all our heart. You may at first be very ignorant of all it implies. God has planted your new heart in the midst of the flesh, the animating principle of which—*self*—has to be denied, to be kept crucified, and by the Holy Spirit put to death. God has placed you in the midst of the world, from which, with all that is of it and its spirit, you are to come out and be entirely separate. God has given you your work in His kingdom, for which He asks all your interest and time and strength. In all three of these respects you need wholeheartedness to enable you to make the sacrifices that may be required.

If you take the ordinary standard of Christian life around you, you will find that wholeheartedness—intense devotion to

God and His service—is hardly thought of. How not to displease God while innocently enjoying as much as possible of this present life is the ruling principle; so the present world ordinarily secures the larger share of interest. To *please self* is considered legitimate and the Christlike life of *not pleasing self* has little place. Wholeheartedness will lead you and enable you to accept Christ's command and to sell all for the pearl of great price. Though at first afraid of what it may involve, do not hesitate to speak the word frequently in the ear of your Father: *with my whole heart.* You may count on the Holy Spirit to open up its meaning—to show you to what service or what sacrifice God calls you in this commitment, to increase its power, to reveal its blessedness, to make it the very spirit of your life of devotion to your Covenant God.*

And now, who is ready to enter into this new and everlasting Covenant with his whole heart? Let each of us do it.

Begin by asking God very humbly to give you, by the Spirit who dwells within, a vision of the heavenly life of wholehearted love and obedience as it has actually been prepared for you in Christ. It is an existing reality, a spiritual endowment out of the life of God which can come upon you. It is secured for you in the Covenant and in Christ Jesus, its Guarantor. Ask earnestly, definitely, believingly, that God will reveal this to you. Rest not until you sense what your Father means you to be, and know with assurance that He has provided accordingly.

When you begin to see why the New Covenant was given, what it promises, and how divinely certain its promises are, *offer yourself to God unreservedly to be taken up into it.* Offer to love Him with your whole heart and to obey Him with all your

---

* For more thought regarding the proper place of *self*, see Note E on page 147.

strength. Do not hold back or be afraid. God has sworn to do you *good* with *His whole heart.* Do not hesitate to say that into *this* Covenant—in which *He promises* to cause you to turn to Him and to love Him with your whole heart—you *now* with your whole heart enter. If there be any fear, just ask again and believingly for a vision of the Covenant life: God swearing to do you good with *His whole heart*; God undertaking to make and enable you to love and obey Him with *your whole heart.* The vision of this life will make you bold to say: "Into this Covenant of a wholehearted love in God and in me, I do with my whole heart now enter. Here will I dwell."

Let us close with this one thought: A redeeming God, rejoicing with His whole heart and whole soul to do us good, and to work in us all that is well-pleasing in His sight—this is the one side. Such is the *God* of the Covenant. Gaze upon Him! Believe Him! Worship Him! Wait upon Him, until the fire begins to burn and your heart is drawn out with all its might to love this God. Then the other side, the human: A redeemed soul, rejoicing with all its heart and all its soul in the love of this God, *you* are entering into the *Covenant of wholehearted love* and venturing to say to Him: "With my whole heart I do love You, God, my exceeding joy."* Such are the children of the Covenant.

Beloved reader, rest not until *you* have entered through Christ the Door into this temple of the love of God.

---

* For more on the whole heart, see Note F on page 150.

Notes

Note A—Chapter Two

The Second Blessing

IN THE LIFE of the believer there sometimes comes a crisis as clearly marked as his conversion—a time at which he passes out of a life of continual feebleness and failure and into a life of strength, victory, and abiding rest. The transition has sometimes been called "the second blessing." Some people have objected to the phrase as being unscriptural, or as tending to make a rule for all what is only a mode of experience in some. Others see it as helping to express clearly in human words what ought to be taught to believers as a possible deliverance from the ordinary life of the Christian into one of abiding fellowship with God and entire devotion to His service. It is my belief that, *rightly understood*, the words express a scriptural truth and may be a help to believers in understanding it.

I have connected "the second blessing" with the two Covenants. Why was it that God made two Covenants—not one, and not three? Because there were two parties concerned. In the first Covenant man was to prove what he could do and what he was. In the second, God would show what He could do. The former spanned a time of needed preparation; the latter, the time of divine fulfillment. Even as this was necessary for the race, it is for the individual. Conversion makes of a sinner a child of God, but one still full of ignorance and weakness, with only a partial conception of what the wholehearted devotion is that God asks of him or of the full possession God is ready to take of him. In some cases the transition from the elementary stage is by gradual growth and enlightenment. But experience teaches that in the great majority of cases this continuous, healthy growth is not found. To those who have never found the secret of victory over sin and perfect rest in God, and have possibly despaired of ever finding it because all their efforts have been failures, it has often been a wonderful help to learn that it is possible by a single decisive step to enter upon an entirely new life.

What is needed to take that step is very simple. The person must see and confess the wrongness, the sin, of the life he is living while not in harmony with God's will. He must see and believe in the life that Scripture holds out, that Christ Jesus promises to work and maintain in him. As he sees that his failure has been owing to his striving in his own strength and believes that our Lord Jesus will actually work *all* in him in divine power, he takes courage and dares surrender himself to Christ anew. Confessing and giving up all that is of self and sin, yielding himself wholly to Christ and His service, he believes and receives a new power to live his life by faith in the Son of God. The change is in many cases as clear, as marked, as wonderful, as conversion. For lack of a better name, "the second blessing" came about most naturally.

When once it is seen how greatly this change is needed in the life of most Christians and how entirely it rests on faith in Christ and His power as revealed in the Word, all doubt as to its scripturalness will be removed. And when once its truth is seen, we shall be surprised to find how throughout Scripture, in both history and teaching, we find what illustrates and confirms it.

Take the twofold passage of Israel through water: first out of Egypt, then into Canaan. The wilderness journey was the result of unbelief and disobedience, allowed by God to humble them and prove them, and to show what was in their heart. When this purpose had been accomplished, a second blessing led them through Jordan into Canaan as mightily as the first had brought them through the Red Sea out of Egypt.

Or, take the Holy Place and the Holy of Holies of the Tabernacle as types of the life in the two Covenants and equally in the two stages of Christian experience. In the former there is very real access to God and fellowship with Him, but always with a veil between. In the latter there is full access through a rent veil into the immediate presence of God and a fuller experience of the power of the heavenly life. As our eyes are opened to see how the average Christian life comes terribly short of God's purpose and how truly the mingled life can be expelled by the power of a new revelation of what God waits to do, the types of Scripture will shine with a new meaning.

Or, look to the teachings of the New Testament. In Romans, Paul contrasts the life of the Christian under the law with that under grace, the spirit of bondage with the spirit brought about by our adoption. What does this mean but that Christians may still be living under the law and its bondage, and that they need to come out of this into a full life of grace and liberty through the Holy Spirit. When one first sees the difference, nothing but the surrender of faith is needed to accept and experience what grace will do by the Holy Spirit.

To the Corinthians, Paul writes of some being carnal and still babes, walking as those after the flesh; others being spiritual, with spiritual discernment and character. To the Galatians he speaks of the liberty with which Christ, by the Spirit, makes one free from the law, in contrast to those who sought to perfect in the flesh what was begun in the Spirit, and who even gloried in the flesh. He calls them to recognize the danger of the carnal, divided life, and to come at once to the life of faith, the life of the Spirit, which alone is according to God's will.

We see throughout Scripture what the state of the Church at the present day confirms: that conversion is only the gate that leads into the path of life, and that inside that gate there is still a great danger of a person's mistaking the path, of turning aside or turning back. Where this has taken place, we are called to turn with our whole heart and to give ourselves to nothing less than all that Christ is willing to work in us. Just as there are many who have always thought that conversion must be slow and gradual and uncertain, and cannot understand how it can be sudden and final—because they take only man's powers into account—so many cannot see how the revelation of the true life of holiness and the entrance into it by faith out of a life of self-effort and failure may be immediate and permanent. They look too much to man's efforts and do not realize that "the second blessing" is nothing more nor less than a new vision of what Christ is willing to work in us and a resultant faith-surrender that yields all to Him.

I would hope that what I have written in this book may

help some to see that "the second blessing" is just what they need. It is what God by His Spirit will work in them and is nothing but the acceptance of Christ in all His saving power as their strength and life. It will bring them into and fit them for a full life in the New Covenant, a life in which God works all in all.

Let me close with a quotation from my Introduction to the book *Dying to Self: A Golden Dialogue*, by William Law:

A great deal has been said against the use of the terms "the Higher Life" and "the Second Blessing." In Law one finds nothing of such language, but of the deep truth of which they are the perhaps defective expression, his book is full. The points on which so much stress is laid in what is called "Keswick teaching" stand out prominently in his whole argument. The low state of the average life of believers, the cause of all failure as coming from self-confidence, the need for an entire surrender of the whole being to the operation of God, the call to turn to Christ as the One and Sure Deliverer from the power of self, the divine certainty of a better life for all who will in self-despair trust Christ for it, and the heavenly joy of a life in which the Spirit of Love fills the heart—these truths are common to both. What makes Law's presentation of the truth of special value is the way in which he shows how humility and utter self-despair, with the resignation to God's mighty working in simple faith, is the infallible way to be delivered from self and have the Spirit of Love born in the heart.

Note B—Chapter Four

The Law Written on the Heart

THE THOUGHT of the law written on the heart sometimes causes difficulty and discouragement because believers do not see or feel in themselves anything corresponding to it. Perhaps an illustration will help to remove the difficulty. There are fluids by which you can write so that nothing is visible, either at once or later, unless the writing is exposed to the sun or the action of some chemical. The writing is there, but one who is ignorant of the process does not realize it is there and does not know how to make it readable. However, a person who is in on the secret will believe it though he does not see it.

It is even thus with the new heart. God has put His law into it. "Blessed are the people in whose heart is God's law." But it is there invisibly. A person who takes God's promise by faith knows that it is in his heart. As long as there is no clear faith on this point, all attempts to find that law or to fulfill it will be vain. But when by simple faith the promise is held fast, the first step is taken to realize it. The soul is then prepared to receive instruction as to what the writing of the law on the heart means. It means, first, that God has implanted in the new heart a love for God's law and a readiness to do all His will. You may not *feel* this disposition there, but it is there. God has put it there. Believe this and be assured that there is in you a divine nature that says (and you, therefore, do not hesitate to say it): "I delight to do Your will, O my God!" (Ps. 40:8). In the name of God, and in faith, *say* it.

This writing of the law means, further, that in planting this principle in you God has taken all that you know of His will already and has inspired that new heart with the readiness to obey it. It may as yet be written there with invisible writing, and you are not conscious of it. That does not matter. You here have to deal with a divine and hidden work of the Holy Spirit. Be not afraid to say: "Oh, how I love Your law!" (Ps. 119:97). God has put the love of Scripture into your heart, the new heart. He has taken away the stony heart; it is by the new heart you have to live.

The next thing implied in this writing of the law is that you have accepted all of God's will—even what you do not yet know—as the delight of your heart. In giving yourself up to God you gave yourself wholly to His will. That was the one condition of your entering the Covenant. Covenant grace will now provide for teaching you to *know*, and strengthening you to *do*, all your Father would have you do.

The whole life in the New Covenant is a life of faith. Faith accepts every promise of the Covenant, is certain that it is being fulfilled, and looks confidently to the God of the Covenant to do His work. Faith believes implicitly in both the promise and the God who gave and fulfills the promise.

It may be well to add here that the same truth holds good for all the promises concerning the new heart—they must be accepted and acted on by faith. When we read of "the love of God shed abroad in the heart by the Holy Spirit," of "loving each other with a clean heart fervently," of "God establishing our heart without blame in holiness," we must, with the eye of faith, regard these spiritual realities as actually and in very deed existing within us. In His hidden, unseen way God is working them there. Not by sight or feeling, but by faith in the living

God and His Word, we know they are governing the dispositions and inclinations of the new heart. In this faith we are to
act, knowing that we have the power to love, to obey, to be
holy. The New Covenant gives us a God who works all in us;
faith in Him gives us the assurance, above and beyond all feeling, that this God is doing His blessed work.

And if the question be asked what we are to think about all
there is within us that contradicts this faith, let us remember
what Scripture teaches us about it. We sometimes speak of having an old and a new heart. Scripture does not do so. It speaks
of the old, the stony, heart, being taken away; of the heart, with
its will, disposition, affections, being made new with a divine
newness. This new heart is placed in the midst of what Scripture calls the flesh, in which there dwells no good thing. We
shall find it a great advantage to adhere as closely as possible to
scriptural language. It will greatly help our faith even to use the
very words God by His Holy Spirit has used to teach us. And it
will greatly clear our view for knowing what to think of the sin
that remains in us if we think of it and deal with it in the light
of God's truth. Every evil desire and affection comes from the
flesh, man's sinful natural life. It owes its power greatly to our
ignorance of its nature and our relying on our own strength to
cast out its evil. I have already pointed out how sinful flesh and
religious flesh are one, and how all failure in the spiritual life is
owing to a secret trust in ourselves. As we accept and make use
of what God says about the flesh, we shall see in it a source of
all evil in us. We shall say of its temptations: "No longer am I
the one doing it, but sin which dwells in me" (Rom. 7:17). We
shall maintain our integrity as we maintain a good conscience—
one that does not condemn us for anything knowingly done
against God's will. And we shall be strong in the faith imparted

by the Holy Spirit, who dwells in the new heart to strengthen it
so that we need not and shall not fulfill the lusts of the flesh.

I conclude with an extract from an address by Rev. F. Webster
at Keswick last year, in confirmation of what I have just said:

> "Put on the Lord Jesus Christ, and make no provision
> for the flesh in regard to its lusts" (Rom. 13:14). Make no
> provision for the flesh. The flesh is there, you know. To deny
> or ignore the existence of an enemy is to give him a great
> chance against you; and the flesh is in the believer to the very
> end, a force of evil to be reckoned with continually. It is an
> evil force inside a man, and yet, thank God, a force which can
> be so dealt with by the power of God that it shall have no
> power to defile the heart or deflect the will. The flesh is in
> you, but your heart may be kept clean moment by moment
> in spite of the existence of evil in your fallen nature. Every
> avenue, every opening that leads into the heart, every thought
> and desire and purpose and imagination of your being, may
> be closed against the flesh, so that there shall be no opportu-
> nity for it to come in and defile the heart or deflect the will
> from the will of God.
>
> You say, "That is a very high standard." But it is the Word
> of God. There is to be no secret sympathy with sin. Although
> the flesh is there, you are to make it no excuse for sins. You
> are not to say, "I am naturally irritable, anxious, jealous, and
> I cannot help letting these things crop up; they come from
> within." Yes, they come from within, but yet there need be no
> provision, no opening in your heart for these things to enter.
> Your heart can be barricaded with an impassable barrier against
> these things. "No provision for the flesh"—not merely the
> front door barred and bolted so that you do not invite them
> to come in, but the side and back door closed too. You may
> be so Christ-possessed and Christ-enclosed that you shall
> positively hate everything that is of the flesh.

"*Make no provision for the flesh.*" The only way to do so is to "put on the Lord Jesus Christ." I spoke of the heart being so barricaded that there would be no entrance to it, that the flesh would never be able to defile it or deflect the will from the will of God. How can that be done? By putting on the Lord Jesus Christ. It has been such a blessing to me just to learn that one secret, just to learn the positive side of deliverance—putting on the Lord Jesus Christ.

Note C—Chapter Seven

George Müller and His Second Conversion

IN THE LIFE of George Müller of Bristol there was an epoch, four years after his conversion, to which he ever after looked back. He often spoke of it as his entrance into the true Christian life.

In an address given to ministers and workers after his ninetieth birthday, he said this:

That leads to another thought—the full surrender of the heart to God. I *was converted* in November 1825, but I only *came into the full surrender of the heart* four years later, in July 1829. The love of money was gone, the love of place was gone, the love of position was gone, the love of worldly pleasures and engagements was gone. God, God, God alone became my portion. I found my all in Him; I wanted nothing else. And by the grace of God this has remained and has made me a happy man, an exceedingly happy man, and it led me to care only about the things of God. I ask, affectionately, my beloved brethren, have you fully surrendered your heart to

God, or is there this thing or that thing with which you are taken up irrespective of God? I read a little of the Scriptures before, but preferred other books; but since that time the revelation He has made of Himself has become unspeakably blessed to me, and I can say from my heart: God is an infinitely lovely Being. Oh, be not satisfied until in your inmost soul you can say: God is an infinitely lovely Being!

The account of this change which he gives in his journal is as follows. He speaks of one whom he had heard preach at Teignmouth, where he had gone for the sake of his health:

> Though I did not like all he said, yet I saw a gravity and solemnity in him different from the rest. Through the instrumentality of this brother the Lord bestowed a great blessing upon me, for which I shall have cause to thank Him throughout eternity. God then began to show me that the Word of God alone is to be our standard of judgment in spiritual things; that it can be explained only by the Holy Spirit, and that in our day, as well as in former times, He is the Teacher of His people. *The office of the Holy Spirit I had not experimentally understood before that time.* I had not before seen that the Holy Spirit alone can teach us about our state by nature, show us our need of a Savior, enable us to believe in Christ, explain to us the Scriptures, help us in preaching, etc.
>
> It was my beginning to understand this point in particular which had a great effect on me; for the Lord enabled me to put it to the test of experience by laying aside commentaries and almost every other book, and simply reading the Word of God and studying. The result of this was that the first evening that I shut myself into my room to give myself to prayer and meditation over the Scriptures, I learned more in a few hours than I had done during a period of several months previously. *But the particular difference was that I received real strength in*

my soul in doing so.

In addition to this, it pleased the Lord to lead me to see a *higher standard of devotedness* than I had seen before. He led me, in a measure, to see what is my glory in this world, even to be despised, to be poor and mean with Christ. . . . I returned to London much better in body. And as to my soul, *the change was so great that it was like a second conversion.*

In another passage he speaks thus:

I fell into the snare into which so many young believers fall, the reading of religious books as preferred to the Scriptures. Now the scriptural way of reasoning would have been: God Himself has condescended to become an author, and I am ignorant of that precious Book which His Holy Spirit has caused to be written; therefore I ought to read again this Book of books most earnestly, most prayerfully, and with much meditation. Instead of acting thus, and being led by my ignorance of the Word to study it more, I let my difficulty of understanding it make me careless of reading it; and then, like many believers, I practically preferred for the first four years of my Christian life the works of uninspired men to the oracles of the living God. The consequence was that I remained a babe, both in knowledge and grace. In knowledge, I say, for all true knowledge must be derived by the Spirit from the Word. This lack of knowledge most sadly kept me back from walking steadily in the ways of God. For it is the truth that makes us free, by delivering us from slavery to the lusts of the flesh, the lusts of the eyes, and the pride of life. The Word proves it, the experience of the saints proves it, and also my own experience most decidedly proves it. For when it pleased the Lord, in August 1829, to bring me really to the Scriptures, my life and walk became very different.

If anyone should ask me how he may read the Scriptures

most profitably, I would advise him:

1. Above all he must seek to have it settled in his own mind *that God alone, by the Holy Spirit, can teach him*, and that, therefore, as God will be inquired for all blessings, it becomes him to seek for God's blessing previous to reading and also while reading.

2. He should also have it settled in his mind that though *the Holy Spirit is the best and sufficient Teacher*, yet He does not always teach immediately when we desire it, and that, therefore, *we may have to entreat Him again and again* for the explanation of certain passages; but that *He will surely teach us* at last, if we will seek for light prayerfully, patiently, and for the glory of God.

Just one more passage, from a eulogy given on the occasion of Müller's ninetieth birthday:

For sixty-nine years and ten months he has been a very happy man. That he attributes to two things. He has maintained a good conscience, not willfully going on in a course he knew to be contrary to the mind of God, he does not, of course, mean that he has been perfect. Secondly, he attributes it to his love of Holy Scripture. Of late years his practice has been four times every year to read through the Scriptures, with application to his own heart and with meditation; and this day he is a greater lover of God's Word than he was sixty-six years ago. It is this, and maintaining a good conscience, that has given him all these years peace and joy in the Holy Ghost.

In connection with what has been said about the New Covenant being a ministry of the Spirit, this narrative is most instructive. It shows us how George Müller's power lay in God's revealing to him the work of the Holy Spirit. He writes that up to the time of that change he had "not experimentally under-stood the office of the Holy Spirit." We speak much of George Müller's power in prayer; it is of importance to remember that that power was entirely owing to his love of, and faith in, God's Word. But it is of still more importance to notice that his power to believe God's Word so fully was entirely owing to his having learned to know the Holy Spirit as his Teacher. When the words of God are explained to us and made living within us by the Holy Spirit, they have a power to awaken faith which they otherwise have not. The Word then brings us into contact with God, comes to us as from God direct, and binds our whole life to Him.

When the Holy Spirit thus feeds us on the Word, our whole life comes under His power, and the fruit is seen not only in the power of prayer but as much in the power of obedience. Notice how Mr. Müller tells us this, that the two secrets of his great happiness were his great *love for God's Word* and his *always maintaining a good conscience*, not knowingly doing anything against the will of God. In giving himself to the teaching of the Holy Spirit, he made a full surrender of his entire heart to God to be ruled by the Word. He gave himself to obey that Word in everything. He believed that the Holy Spirit gave the grace to obey, and so he was able to maintain a walk free from knowingly transgressing God's law. This is a point he always insisted on. So he writes, in regard to a life of dependence upon God: "It will not do—it is not possible—*to live in sin* and at the same time, by communion with God, to draw down from heaven everything one needs for the life that now is." Again, speaking of the strengthening of faith: "It is of the utmost importance that we seek to maintain *an upright heart and a good conscience*, and therefore do not knowingly and habitually indulge in those things that are contrary to the mind of God. All my confidence in God, all my leaning upon Him in the hour of trial, will be gone if I have a guilty conscience and do not seek to put away this guilty conscience but still continue to do things that are contrary to His mind."

A careful perusal of this testimony will show us how the chief points usually insisted upon in connection with "the second blessing" are all found here. There is the full surrender of the heart to be taught and led alone by the Spirit of God. There is the higher standard of holiness which is at once set up. There is the tender desire to offend God in nothing, but to have at all times a good conscience that testifies that we are pleasing to God. And there is the faith that where the Holy Spirit reveals to us in the Word the will of God, He gives the sufficient strength for the doing of it. "The particular difference," he says, of reading with faith in the Holy Spirit's teaching, "was that I received real strength in my soul in doing so." No wonder that he said: "*The change was so great that it was like a second conversion.*"

All centers in this, that we believe in the New Covenant and its promises as a ministry of the Spirit. That belief may come to some suddenly, as to George Müller; or it may dawn upon others by degrees. Let all say to God that they are ready to put their whole heart and life under the rule of the Holy Spirit dwelling in them, teaching them by the Word and strengthening them by His grace. He enables us to live lives pleasing to God.

Note D—Chapter Ten

Canon Battersby

I DOUBT if I can find a better case by which to illustrate the place Christ, the Mediator of the Covenant, takes in leading into its full blessing than that of the founder of the Keswick Convention, the late Canon Battersby.

It was at the Oxford Convention in 1873 that he witnessed to having "received a new and distinct blessing to which I had been a stranger before." For more than twenty-five years he had been most diligent as a minister of the gospel, and, as appears from his journals, most faithful in seeking to maintain a close walk with God. But he was ever disturbed by the consciousness of being overcome by sin. As far back as 1853 he had written, "I feel again how very far I am from enjoying habitually that peace and love and joy which Christ promises. I must confess that I have it not, and that very ungentle and unchristian tempers often strive within me for the mastery." When in 1873 he read what was being published of the "higher life," the effect was to render him utterly dissatisfied with himself and his state. There were indeed difficulties he could not quite understand in that teaching, but he felt that he must either reach forward to better things—nothing less than redemption from *all* iniquities—or fall back more and more into worldliness and sin.

At Oxford he heard an address on "the rest of faith." It opened his eyes to the truth that a believer who really longs for deliverance from sinning must simply take Christ at His word and, without feeling, reckon on Him to do His work of cleansing and keeping the soul. "I thought of the sufficiency of Jesus, and said, 'I *will rest* in Him'; and I did rest in Him. I was afraid lest it should be a passing emotion; but I found that a presence of Jesus was graciously manifested to me in a way I knew not before, and that *I did abide in Him.* I do not want to rest in these emotions, but just to believe and to cling to Christ as my all." He was a man of very reserved nature but felt it a duty before the close of the Conference to publicly confess his past shortcoming and to testify openly to his having entered upon a new and definite experience.

In a paper written not long after this he pointed out what the steps are leading to this experience. First, there must be a clear view of the possibilities of Christian attainment: a life in word and action habitually governed by the Spirit, in constant communion with God, and continual victory over sin through abiding in Christ. Then, there must follow the deliberate purpose of the will for a full renunciation of all the idols of the flesh or spirit and a will-surrender to Christ. And then comes this last and important step: *We must look up to and wait upon our ascended Lord for all that we need to enable us to do this.*

A careful perusal of this very brief statement will prove how everything centered here in Christ. The surrender for a life of continual communion and victory is to be to Christ. The strength for that life is to be in Him and from Him, by faith in Him. And *the power* to make the full surrender and rest in Him *is to be waited for from Him alone.*

In June 1875 the first Keswick Convention was held. In the circular announcing it, we read: "Many are everywhere thirsting that they may be brought to enjoy more of the divine presence in their daily life, and a fuller manifestation of the Holy Spirit's power, whether in subduing the lusts of the flesh or in enabling them to offer more effective service to God. It is certainly God's will that His children should be satisfied in regard to these longings; and there are those who can testify that He can satisfy them, and does satisfy them with daily fresh manifestations of His grace and power." The results of the very first Convention were most blessed, so that after its close he wrote: "There is a very remarkable resemblance in the testimonies I have since received as to the nature of the blessing obtained, viz., *the ability given* to make a full surrender to the Lord and the consequent experience of an abiding peace, far exceeding anything previously experienced." Through all, the chief thought was *Christ*, first drawing and enabling the soul to rest in Him and then meeting it with the fulfillment of its desire, the abiding experience of His power to keep it in victory over sin and in communion with God.

And what was the fruit of this new experience? Eight years later Canon Battersby spoke: "It is now eight years since I knew this blessing as my own. I cannot say that I have never for a moment ceased to trust the Lord to keep me. But I can say that so long as I have trusted Him, He has kept me; He has been faithful."

Note E—Chapter Eighteen

Nothing of Myself

O NE WOULD think that nothing could be made plainer than the meaning of the New Covenant—that everything is to be done by God Himself. And yet believers and even teachers frequently do not take it in. And even those who do, find it hard to live it out. It is as though our whole being is blind to the true working of God. It is so far beyond human conception that our little hearts cannot rise to the reality of His infinite love making itself one with us, and delighting to dwell in us and work in us all that has to be done there. We find that when we think we have accepted the truth, we treat it as only an abstract idea. We are such strangers to a true knowledge of God.

Not long ago I had occasion to make a study of the Gospel of John and of the life of our Lord as set forth there. I cannot say how deeply I was impressed once again with what I cannot but regard as the deepest secret of Christ's life on earth, *His dependence on the Father.* It has come to me like a new revelation. Some twelve or more times He uses the word *not* and *nothing* of Himself: *Not* My will, *not* My words, *not* My honor, *not* My own glory; I can do *nothing* of Myself; I speak *not* of Myself; I came *not* of Myself; I do *nothing* of Myself.

Just think a moment what this means in connection with what He tells us of His life in the Father. "Just as the Father has life in Himself, even so He gave to the Son also to have life in Himself" (5:26). "So that all will honor the Son even as they honor the Father" (5:23). And yet this Son, who has life in

Himself even as the Father has, immediately adds (5:30): "I can do nothing on My own initiative." We would have thought that with this life in Himself He would have the right of independent action as the Father has. But no. "The Son can do *nothing* of Himself, unless it is something He sees the Father doing" (5:19). The chief mark of the life of Christ was, evidently, unceasing dependence—receiving from the Father, by the moment, what He had to speak or do.

Nothing of Myself is manifestly as true of Him as it ever could be of the weakest man. The more closely we study this truth, and Christ's life in the light of it, the more we are compelled to say that the deepest root of Christ's relationship to the Father—the true reason why He was so well-pleasing, the secret of His glorifying the Father—was this: *He allowed the Father to do all in Him.* His whole attitude was that of the open ear, the servant spirit, the childlike dependence that waited for all on the Father.

The infinite importance of this truth in the Christian life is easily felt. The life Christ lived in the Father is the life He imparts to us. We are to abide in Him and He in us, *even as* He abides in the Father and the Father in Him. And if the secret of His abiding in the Father be this unceasing self-denial—"I can do nothing on My own initiative"—then absolute dependence and waiting upon God must surely be the most marked feature of our Christian life and the all-pervading disposition we seek to maintain. We must die to self to sink down in humility, meekness, patience, and resignation to God, in order to have the birth of divine love in our souls. Entire self-renunciation was not merely one of many virtues in the character of Christ; indeed, it was the essential one, without which the Father could have accomplished nothing through Him.

Let us make Christ's words our own: "*By myself I can accomplish nothing—I can do nothing on my own.*" Take it as the keynote of a single day. Look up and see the infinite God waiting to do everything as soon as we are ready to give up all to Him and receive all from Him. Bow down in lowly worship, and wait for the Holy Spirit to work some measure of the mind of Christ in you. Do not be disconcerted if you do not learn the lesson at once; the God of love is waiting to do everything in the one who is willing to be nothing. At moments the teaching appears dangerous, at other times terribly difficult. The Blessed Son of God teaches it to us—this was His whole life: I can do nothing on My own. *He* is our life; *He* will work it in us. And when, as the Lamb of God, He shapes His disposition in us, we shall be prepared for Him to rise on us and shine in us in His heavenly glory.

"Nothing on My own initiative"—that word spoken eighteen hundred years ago, coming out of the inmost depths of the heart of the Son of God—is a seed in which the power of eternal life is hidden. Take it straight from the heart of Christ and hide it in your heart. Meditate on it until it reveals the beauty of His divine meekness and humility and explains how all the power and glory of God could work in Him. Believe in this truth as containing the very life and disposition which you need, and believe in Christ whose Spirit dwells in the seed to make it true in you. Begin, in single acts of self-emptying, to offer these words to God as the one desire of your heart. Count upon God accepting them and meeting them with His grace, to make the acts into habits and the habits into dispositions. And you may depend upon it—there is nothing that will lift you so near to God, nothing that will unite you closer to Christ, nothing that will prepare you for the abiding presence and power of God working in you, as will the death to self which is found in the simple concept: *Nothing on my own.*

This principle is one of the keys to the New Covenant life. As I believe that God is actually to work all in me, I shall see that the one thing that is hindering me is my doing something by myself. As I am willing to learn from Christ by the Holy Spirit to say truly, *Nothing on my own,* I shall have the true preparation to receive all God has engaged to work, and the power confidently to expect it. I shall learn that the whole secret of the New Covenant is just one thing: *God works all!* The seal of the Covenant stands sure: "I, the Lord, have spoken it, and I will do it."

Note F—Chapter Eighteen

The Whole Heart

LET ME give the principal passages in which the words "the whole heart" or "all the heart" are used. A careful study of them will show how wholehearted love and service is what God has always asked, because He can, in the very nature of things, ask nothing less. The prayerful and believing acceptance of the words will awaken the assurance that such wholehearted love and service is exactly the blessing the New Covenant was meant to make possible. That assurance will prepare us for turning to the omnipotence of God to work in us what may have hitherto appeared beyond our reach.

Hear, first, God's word in Deuteronomy:

4:29: "But from there you will seek the Lord your God, and you will find Him if you search for Him with all your heart and all your soul."

6:4–5: "Hear, O Israel! The Lord is our God, the Lord is one! You shall love the Lord your God with all your heart and with all your soul and with all your might."

10:12: "What does the Lord your God require from you, but to fear the Lord your God, to walk in all His ways and love Him, and to serve the Lord your God with all your heart and with all your soul."

11:13: "Listen obediently to My commandments which I am commanding you today, to love the Lord your God and to serve Him with all your heart and all your soul."

13:3: "The Lord your God is testing you to find out if you love the Lord your God with all your heart and with all your soul."

26:16: "You shall therefore be careful to do them with all your heart and with all your soul."

30:6: "The Lord your God will circumcise your heart . . . to love the Lord your God with all your heart and with all your soul" (see also vv. 9–10).

Take these oft-repeated words as the expression of God's will concerning His people and concerning yourself; ask if you could wish to give God anything less. Take the last-cited verse as the divine promise of the New Covenant—that He will circumcise, will so cleanse the heart to love Him with a whole-hearted love, that obedience is within your reach; and declare whether or not you will dedicate yourself afresh to keep this, His first and great commandment.

Listen to Joshua (22:5): "Be very careful . . . to love the

Lord your God and walk in all His ways and to keep His commandments and hold fast to Him and serve Him with all your heart and with all your soul."

Listen to Samuel (1 Sam. 12:20, 24): "Do not turn aside from following the Lord, but serve the Lord with all your heart. Only fear the Lord and serve Him in truth with all your heart."

Hear David repeating God's promise to Solomon (1 Kings 2:4): "If your sons are careful of their way, to walk before Me in truth with all their heart and with all their soul. . . ."

Hear God's word concerning David (1 Kings 14:8): "My servant David . . . who followed Me with all his heart, to do only that which was right in My sight."

Hear Solomon in his temple prayer (1 Kings 8:48–49): "If they return to You with all their heart and with all their soul . . . then hear their prayer."

Listen to what is said of Jehu (2 Kings 10:30–31): "The Lord said to Jehu, 'Because you have done well in executing what is right in My eyes . . . .' But Jehu was not careful to walk in the law of the Lord, the God of Israel, with all his heart."

Of Josiah we read (2 Kings 23:3, 25): "The king stood by the pillar and made a covenant before the Lord, to walk after the Lord . . . with all his heart and with all his soul, to carry out the words of this covenant that were written in this book. . . . Before him there was no king like him who turned to the Lord with all his heart and with all his soul and with all his might."

Of Asa and his people we read (2 Chron. 15:12): "They entered into the covenant to seek the Lord God of their fathers with all their heart and soul."

Of Jehoshaphat, men said (2 Chron. 22:9): "He sought the Lord with all his heart."

And of Hezekiah it is written (2 Chron. 31:21): "Every work

which he began in the service of . . . his God, he did it with all his heart and prospered."

Oh, that all would ask God to give them, by the Holy Spirit, a simple vision of Himself!—claiming, giving, accepting, blessing, delighting in, the love and service of the whole heart. Surely they would fall down and join the ranks of those who have given it, and would refuse to think of anything as true religious life or worship or service other than that in which their whole heart went out to God.

Turn to the Psalms. Hear David (9:1, 111:1, 138:1): "I will give thanks to the Lord with all my heart." And read in Psalm 119, the psalm of the way of blessedness: "Blessed are those who seek Him with all their heart. . . . With all my heart I have sought You. . . . Give me understanding, that I may observe Your law, and keep it with all my heart. . . . I entreated Your favor with all my heart"—praise and prayer, seeking God and keeping His precepts, all equally with the whole heart.

As we see men engaged in their earthly pursuits in search of money, or pleasure, or fame, or power *with their whole heart,* should we not ask: Is this the spirit in which Christians consider that God must be served? Is this the spirit in which I serve Him? Rather, is this not the one thing needful in our religion: Lord, reveal unto us Your will?

Now, just a few words more from the Prophets about the new time, the great change that can come into our lives:

Jeremiah 24:7: I will give them a heart to know Me, for I am the Lord; and they will be My people, and I will be their God, for they will return to Me with their whole heart."

29:13–14: " 'You will seek Me and find Me when you search for Me with all your heart. I will be found by you,' declares the Lord."

32:39–41. Let my reader not be weary of reading carefully these divine words; they contain the secret, the seed, the living power of a complete transition out of a life in the bondage of half-hearted service to the glorious liberty of the children of God: "I will give them one heart and one way, that they may fear Me always. . . . I will make an everlasting covenant with them that I will not turn away from them, to do them good; and I will put the fear of Me in their hearts so that they will not turn away from Me. I will rejoice over them to do them good . . . with all My heart and all My soul."

It is to be all God's doing. And He is to do it with all His heart and all His soul. It is the vision of this God with His whole heart loving us, longing and delighting to fulfill His promise and make us wholly His own, that we need. *This vision makes it impossible not to love Him with our whole heart.* Lord, open our eyes that we may see!

Joel 2:12: " 'Yet even now,' declares the Lord, 'return to Me with all your heart.'"

Zephaniah 3:14–15: "Shout in triumph, O Israel! Rejoice and exult with all your heart, O daughter of Jerusalem! The Lord has taken away His judgments against you, He has cleared away your enemies. The King of Israel, the Lord, is in your midst; you will fear disaster no more."

Now one word from our Lord Jesus (Matt. 22:37): "He said to him, 'You shall love the Lord your God with all your heart. . . .'" This is the great and foremost commandment. This is the sum of the law that Jesus came to fulfill for us and in us— *came to enable us to fulfill.* "For what the law could not do, weak as it was through the flesh, God did: sending His own Son . . . He condemned sin in the flesh, so that the requirement of the law might be fulfilled in us . . . who walk according to the

Spirit" (Rom. 8:3–4).

Praise God! this requirement of the law—loving God with all the heart, for love is the fulfilling of the law—this requirement of the law is fulfilled in us as we walk according to the Spirit. Jesus came to make it possible. He gives His Spirit—the Spirit of life in Christ Jesus—to make it actual. Let us not fear to give ourselves as a whole burnt-offering, acceptable to God—loving Him with all our heart and mind and strength.

May I ask the reader just once again to peruse Chapter 6 on "The Everlasting Covenant" and Chapter 18 on "Entering the Covenant: With All the Heart." And ask, then, if you have not yet entered fully into this Covenant with your whole heart, whether you are not ready to do it now. God demands, God works. God is so infinitely worthy of the whole heart! Fear not to say He shall have it. You may confidently count upon the blessed Lord Jesus, the Guarantor of the Covenant—whose responsibilty it is to make it true in you by His Spirit—to enable you to exercise the faith that knows that God's power will work what He has promised. In His name say: "With my whole heart I do love You!"

This book was produced by CLC Publications. We hope it has been life-changing and has given you a fresh experience of God through the work of the Holy Spirit. CLC Publications is an outreach of CLC Ministries International, a global literature mission with work in over 50 countries. If you would like to know more about us or are interested in opportunities to serve with a faith mission, we invite you to contact us at:

CLC Ministries International
P.O. Box 1449
Fort Washington, PA 19034

—

Phone: (215) 542-1242
E-mail: clcmail@clcusa.org
Websites: www.clcusa.org
www.clcpublications.com

- - - - - - - - - - - - - - - - -

DO YOU LOVE GOOD CHRISTIAN BOOKS?
Do you have a heart for worldwide missions?

You can receive a FREE subscription to:

Floodtide

(CLC's magazine on global literature missions).

Order by e-mail at:

floodtide@clcusa.org
or fill in the coupon below and mail to:

P.O. Box 1449
Fort Washington, PA 19034

- -

FREE FLOODTIDE SUBSCRIPTION!

Name: _____

Address: _____

_____

Phone: _____ E-mail: _____

READ THE REMARKABLE STORY OF
the founding of
CLC INTERNATIONAL

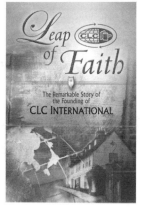

Andrew Murray,
The
Authorized Biography

by
Leona Choy

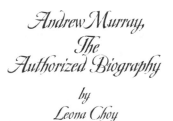

"Why has the Lord put me in ministry— unfit as I am? Why can't I find the strength I need?"

These were some of the questions Andrew Murray struggled with as a young pastor. What experiences changed him into the great man of faith whose writings have affected millions?

A 19th-century missionary statesman, revivalist, evangelist, and pastor, Andrew Murray is one of the best-loved and most widely read writers on the deeper life. Many of today's readers, however, are unaware of the struggles and steps of faith which molded this servant of God into an exceptional teacher of faith, prayer, and Spirit-filled living.

ISBN 0-87508-829-5

The
Spiritual Life
by Andrew Murray

Practical, Biblical advice on allowing the Holy Spirit complete control over your life.

In a series of messages given at Moody Bible Institute in 1895, Andrew Murray showed the way to living a Spirit-filled life. *The Spiritual Life*, the book derived from these messages, is wise and timely counsel from a veteran saint and a journeyman in the life of faith. In an era when discussion of the deeper life is often met with indifference or extremism, Murray brings a healthy balance.

ISBN 0-87508-696-9

Let Us Draw Near by *Andrew Murray*

Has
 Your
  Spiritual
   Growth
    Stagnated?

Do
 You
  Lack
   Spiritual
    Power?

Today's church faces many of the same problems as the Hebrew church of the first century. There is little growth and a lack of spiritual power coming from not knowing or understanding Jesus accurately.

Andrew Murray reveals how knowing the timeless truths of the divinity and humanity of our Lord, His heavenly Priesthood, and our access to God's Presence, helps increase our faith and enables us to dwell in God's presence as He intended.

*Come discover the treasures contained
in the book of Hebrews, as Murray teaches us:*

• *The Four Great Blessings of the New Life*
• *The Four Key Marks of the True Believer*
• *The Four Great Responsibilities of the Opened Sanctuary*

ISBN 0-87508-772-8